Deductive Thinking Skills

SERIES TITLES

Mind Benders®

Book 1 • Book 2 • Verbal

Book 3 • Book 4 • Book 5 • Book 6 • Book 7 • Book 8

Written by
Anita Harnadek

Graphics by
Karla Garrett
Scott Slyter

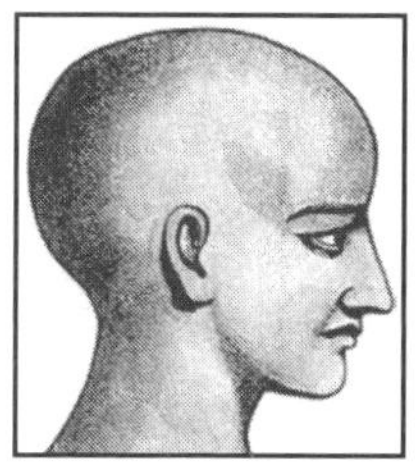

THE CRITICAL THINKING CO.™
www.CriticalThinking.com
Phone: 800-458-4849 • Fax: 831-393-3277
P.O. Box 1610 • Seaside • CA 93955-1610
ISBN 978-1-60144-307-6

Printed in the United States of America by McNaughton & Gunn, Inc., Saline, MI (Jan. 2011)

TABLE OF CONTENTS

TEACHING SUGGESTIONS

PURPOSE

The *Mind Benders®* series improves deductive reasoning, reading comprehension skills, and organized analysis skills.

GENERAL INFORMATION

There are nine books in this series:

Book 1, PreK-K
Book 2, Grades 1-2
Verbal, Grades K-2
Book 3, Grades 3-6
Book 4, Grades 3-6
Book 5, Grades 7-12+
Book 6, Grades 7-12+
Book 7, Grades 7-12+
Book 8, Grades 7-12+

Books 1 and 2 are the easiest level and are often used to introduce students (as young as preschool) to *Mind Benders®* problems and charts.

The *Verbal* book has easy problems with a handful of medium problems, designed for auditory use.

Books 3 and 4 are easy, and Books 7 and 8 are difficult. Books 5 and 6 are medium-level difficulty.

About the Clues in MIND BENDERS®

In general, the *Mind Benders®* clues are based on general standards and customs found in the U.S. society as a whole. Therefore, use common sense and context in deciding what the clues mean.

For example:

a. Assume that only males have traditionally male names (John, Robert, Dave) and only females have traditionally female names (Mary, Jennifer, Cathy). But be careful not to make such assumptions about unisex names (Pat, Chris).

b. Assume that typical U.S. social relationships apply. For example, if John is engaged to Mary, you may assume they know each other. You may assume that very close relatives know each other.

c. Don't assume that rare age relationships may apply. For example, don't assume that a 7-year-old might be a college graduate, or that a parent might be younger than his or her adopted child. On the other hand, more common age relationships can apply. A husband may be a good deal younger than his wife, or a 45-year-old may get the mumps.

d. Assume that animals are of normal size. For example, "a horse" is not "a pygmy horse"; "a small dog" is smaller than a goat; a "large dog" is simply one of the larger breeds of dogs. If a problem talks about a cat and a fox, assume that the cat is smaller than the fox. Do not think that maybe the cat is fully grown and the fox is a few weeks old.

e. Assume that animals are called by their usual names within the context of the information given. For example, if John and Mary have a pet dog and a pet cat, assume that the cat is an ordinary household cat, rather than maybe a tiger or a leopard.

f. Don't look for tricky, misleading situations. For example, suppose the problem has four houses in a row (and no other houses). And suppose Debby lives next door to Gary. Don't assume that Debby or Gary might live in a garage between two of the houses. Assume that they live in two of the four houses in the problem.

g. Pay attention to what the clues say, and assume that typical U.S. social norms apply. For example:

(1) If a problem has four people, and one clue says, "Cathy and the dentist ride to work together in a car pool," and another clue says, "Brown, who does not know any of the other three people, is not the typist," then you should deduce that neither Cathy nor the dentist is Brown.

(2) "Neither Bob nor Young lives in the white house," means, "Bob is not Young, and Bob does not live in the white house, and Young does not live in the white house."

(3) "John and Abbott went bowling with Dave and Smith," means, "Four different people went bowling together. One of these was John, one was Abbott, one was Dave, and one was Smith."

(4) "Jane doesn't know either Mary or the artist," means, "Jane doesn't know Mary, and Jane doesn't know the artist, and Mary is not the artist."

(5) "Neither Carol nor Bill went to the party, and Norris didn't go, either," refers to three different people.

(6) In general, "neither ... nor" and "either ... or" sentences will refer to separate things, as in the above examples. Just plain "or" sentences, however, are sometimes less definite, as in this example: "Neither Becky nor Jackson has the dog or is the secretary." Here, Becky and Jackson are different people, but we aren't sure that the person who has the dog is not also the secretary.

How to Solve a Multi-Dimensional *Mind Bender*®

Read the sample problem and use the multi-dimensional chart to solve it.

Sample Problem

Jim, Jason, and Tom have last names Smith, Lyons, and Dutcher. Each boy has a favorite sport (soccer, tennis, and fishing). Read the clues to find each boy's last name and favorite sport.

1. Jason plays his favorite sport by himself, but also plays Dutcher's favorite sport, tennis.
2. Lyons knows Tom, but they don't play any sports together.

	Smith	Lyons	Dutcher	soccer	tennis	fishing
Jim						
Jason						
Tom						
soccer						
tennis						
fishing						

Clue 1 tells us that Jason plays his favorite sport by himself. Since tennis and soccer require other players, Jason's favorite sport must be fishing. Mark all these answers on the chart (1a).

Clue 1 also tells us that Jason plays Dutcher's favorite sport: tennis. This tells us Dutcher's favorite sport and that Jason's last name is not Dutcher. Mark all these answers on the chart (1b).

	Smith	Lyons	Dutcher	soccer	tennis	fishing
Jim						1a –
Jason			1b –	1a –	1a –	1a +
Tom		2a –				1a –
soccer			1b –			
tennis	1b –	1b –	1b +			
fishing			1b –			

Clue 2 tells us that Lyons knows Tom, but they don't play any sports together. This tells us that Tom's last name is not Lyons, so mark this answer on the chart (2a).

Clue 2 also states that Lyons and Tom don't play any sports together. This fact, along with the fact that Jason plays with Dutcher, tells us that Jason's last name is not Lyons. Mark all these answers on the chart (2b).

If Jason's last name isn't Dutcher or Lyons, then it must be Smith. If Tom isn't Smith or Lyons, then he must be Dutcher. If Jason is Smith, and Tom is Dutcher, then Jim's last name must be Lyons. Mark all these answers on the chart (2b). If Dutcher is Tom, then Dutcher plays tennis and Jason Smith is the fisherman. Jim Lyons is the soccer player. Mark all these answers on the chart (2b).

	Smith	Lyons	Dutcher	soccer	tennis	fishing
Jim	2b –	2b +	2b –	2b +	2b –	1a –
Jason	2b +	2b –	1b –	1a –	1a –	1a +
Tom	2b –	2a –	2b +	2b –	2b +	1a –
soccer	2b –	2b +	1b –			
tennis	1b –	1b –	1b +			
fishing	2b +	2b –	1b –			

Pets at Home

Four children (Ed, Marie, Natalie, and Quentin) are different ages (9, 10, 11, and 13), have different pets (cat, dog, gerbil, and parakeet), and live in different kinds of houses (aluminum siding, brick, frame, and stucco). Read the clues to find each child's age, pet, and kind of house.

1. Ed and the cat's owner play on the same team in Little League baseball.
2. Marie and the gerbil's owner live next door to each other.
3. The dog owner is two years older than the girl who lives in the house with aluminum siding.
4. The 11-year-old lives a block away from Quentin, who does not live in the frame house.
5. The parakeet owner's parents won't let her play football.
6. The brick house is two blocks from the 9-year-old's house.
7. Natalie, Marie, and the 11-year-old sometimes walk to school together.
8. The 10-year-old is a girl.
9. The cat owner is younger than the person who lives in the stucco house but is older than Marie.

	9	10	11	13	cat	dog	gerbil	parakeet	aluminum siding	brick	frame	stucco
Ed												
Marie												
Natalie												
Quentin												
cat												
dog												
gerbil												
parakeet												
aluminum siding												
brick												
frame												
stucco												

Their Favorite Things

Ada, Brian, Carmella, and Daniel live in Maine, Nebraska, Oregon, and Pennsylvania. Their last names are Eaton, Farmer, Grey, and Hill. Their favorite foods are Idaho potatoes, jam, kidney beans, and lemon pie. Their favorite colors are red, salmon, tan, and umber. Read the clues to find each person's full name, favorite food, favorite color, and state.

1. Ada and Eaton live in the East.
2. Hill and Carmella don't like sweet foods.
3. Daniel and Farmer don't like brownish colors.
4. The man who lives in Maine went to school with Brian.
5. The Nebraskan doesn't like reddish colors.
6. Hill's favorite color doesn't have any of the same letters as her full name.
7. Carmella doesn't like red, but that's the lemon pie eater's favorite color.
8. Eaton's favorite food is not lemon pie.
9. The kidney bean eater does not live in Nebraska.

	Eaton	Farmer	Grey	Hill	Idaho potatoes	jam	kidney beans	lemon pie	Maine	Nebraska	Oregon	Pennsylvania	red	salmon	tan	umber
Ada																
Brian																
Camella																
Daniel																
Idaho potatoes																
jam																
kidney beans																
lemon pie																
Maine																
Nebraska																
Oregon																
Pennsylvania																
red																
salmon																
tan																
umber																

Unusual Animals

Four animals (a cat, a dog, an elephant, and a tiger) are all of normal size but are still somewhat unusual. Each has a dominant color (green, purple, red, and rust), and the hair or hide of each has an overall pattern (checkered, plaid, polka-dotted, and striped). Their names are Fido, King, Princess, and Tiny. Their ages are 1, 3, 6, and 20 years. They live in Africa, Australia, Europe, and India. Read the clues to find each kind of animal, color, pattern, name, age, and where it lives.

1. The product of the ages of the elephant and the African animal is 20.
2. The green animal is often thought of as being the same kind of animal as King, but on a larger scale.
3. The sum of the ages of the purple animal, the cat, and the checkered animal is 10.
4. The sum of the ages of the cat and the plaid animal is 23.
5. The sum of the ages of the tiger, Fido, and the animal from Africa is 27.
6. The product of the ages of Tiny and the striped animal is 6.
7. The sum of the ages of Fido, the rust-colored animal, and the European animal is 29.
8. The polka-dotted animal liked its own color, but it thought the Indian animal's color ridiculous.

	green	purple	red	rust	checkered	plaid	polka-dotted	striped	Fido	King	Princess	Tiny	1	3	6	20	Africa	Australia	Europe	India
cat																				
dog																				
elephant																				
tiger																				
checkered																				
plaid																				
polka-dotted																				
striped																				
Fido																				
King																				
Princess																				
Tiny																				
1																				
3																				
6																				
20																				
Africa																				
Australia																				
Europe																				
India																				

All Sick

Andrea, Barry, Charlene, and Darrell, whose last names are Ewell, Farrell, Gorton, and Hunter, are all in elementary school (grades 1, 2, 4, and 5) and all had an illness (chicken pox, flu, measles, and mumps) at the same time. Their teachers are Ilger, Jones, Kay, and Lorry. Their best subjects are arithmetic, music, reading, and spelling. Read the clues to find each student's full name, grade, illness, teacher, and best subject.

1. The boys have women teachers, and the girls have men teachers.
2. Farrell, who had measles, and the Gorton boy are in the highest grades.
3. Ms. Jones' student and the student whose best subject is arithmetic are in the lowest grades.
4. Music is not the best subject of either Barry or Charlene.
5. Ewell likes his teacher better than the second grade teacher or Mr. Kay.
6. Barry is four grades behind the boy who had the flu.
7. Lorry's student had mumps.
8. The fifth-grader's best subject is spelling.

	Ewell	Farrell	Gorton	Hunter	1	2	4	5	chicken pox	flu	measles	mumps	Ilger	Jones	Kay	Lorry	arithmetic	music	reading	spelling
Andrea																				
Barry																				
Charlene																				
Darrell																				
1																				
2																				
4																				
5																				
chicken pox																				
flu																				
measles																				
mumps																				
Ilger																				
Jones																				
Kay																				
Lorry																				
arithmetic																				
music																				
reading																				
spelling																				

Appointments

Ardith, Brady, Celeste, and Ethan each had an appointment yesterday morning (9:00, 9:30, 10:00, and 11:00) with a professional person (dentist, lawyer, physician, and veterinarian). The last names of the four people who had the appointments are Frampton, Gardner, Humphrey, and Ippman. The last names of the professional people are Jackson, Manning, Norton, and Roberts. Read the clues to find each person's full name, appointment time, and name and profession of person seen at the appointment. The clues below describe normal conditions of a professional visit. (For example, the lawyer did not put a filling in a tooth.)

1. Frampton had car trouble and was slightly late for her appointment.
2. Brady and Ardith kept their appointments on time, and Norton's client was slightly early.
3. Gardner's appointment was after the appointment with the dentist and before the appointment with Manning.
4. The appointment with Ms. Jackson was earlier than Humphrey's appointment.
5. Ippman had a vaccination during her appointment.
6. Roberts and the physician had lunch together two days ago.
7. Ethan's appointment was not at 9:30.
8. Brady's appointment was not with the lawyer.

	Frampton	Gardner	Humphrey	Ippman	dentist	lawyer	physician	veterinarian	Jackson	Manning	Norton	Roberts	9:00	9:30	10:00	11:00
Ardith																
Brady																
Celeste																
Ethan																
dentist																
lawyer																
physician																
veterinarian																
Jackson																
Manning																
Norton																
Roberts																
9:00																
9:30																
10:00																
11:00																

Names and Occupations

Four men (Aston, Basil, Cary, and Derek) work as a roofer, a secretary, a truck driver, and an upholsterer. Their wives (Edwina, Felicia, Genevieve, and Heather) work as a mathematician, a nurse, an osteopath, and a professor. Their last names are Idwell, Jacobs, Kroman, and Lawton. Read the clues to find each person's full name and occupation.

1. Felicia called Mrs. Jacobs to ask if the nurse was visiting her.
2. Mr. Lawton and the truck driver went with Edwina and the nurse, their wives, to a concert last night.
3. Cary, the secretary, and Mr. Kroman all went downtown with Felicia and the mathematician this morning.
4. Derek's wife invited the osteopath and the professor to a church picnic.
5. Heather told her husband that Basil and Mr. Idwell helped her carry packages this morning.
6 The secretary, Heather, Mr. Idwell, and the osteopath played duplicate bridge from early evening until late last night.
7. The roofer's wife and the osteopath saw Heather and the professor today.
8. Basil is not married to Edwina.

	Aston	Basil	Cary	Derek	roofer	secretary	truck driver	upholsterer	Edwina	Felicia	Genevieve	Heather	mathematician	nurse	osteopath	professor
Idwell																
Jacobs																
Kroman																
Lawton																
roofer																
secretary																
truck driver																
upholsterer																
Edwina																
Felicia																
Genevieve																
Heather																
mathematician																
nurse																
osteopath																
professor																

Downtown Shopping

Arthur, Bertha, Carlo, and Donna, whose last names are Eggleston, Friar, Gaucher, and Hinnel, each went shopping at a different place (downtown, a local store, a shopping mall, and a small group of stores). The distances of their homes from the stores are 1 block, 3 miles, 5 miles, and 10 miles. Their transportation means were a bus, the family car, jogging, and a neighbor's car. Each person purchased only one kind of item (lumber, power mower, shorts, and slacks). Read the clues to find each person's full name, shopping place, distance traveled, transportation, and item purchased.

1. Eggleston's purchase was too heavy and clumsy for her to manage alone, so she went with a neighbor in the neighbor's car.
2. Gaucher, who did not go to the local store, wore his purchase home.
3. The shopping mall was closer than the store where the slacks were bought but farther than the store where the jogger went.
4. The man who bought the lumber did not go as far as the jogger.
5. Bertha went farther than Hinnel but only half as far as the woman who took the bus downtown.
6. Carlo did not buy the shorts.

	Eggleston	Friar	Gaucher	Hinnel	downtown	local store	shopping mall	group of stores	1 block	3 miles	5 miles	10 miles	bus	family car	jogging	neighbor's car	lumber	power mower	shorts	slacks
Arthur																				
Bertha																				
Carlo																				
Donna																				
downtown																				
local store																				
shopping mall																				
group of stores																				
1 block																				
3 miles																				
5 miles																				
10 miles																				
bus																				
family car																				
jogging																				
neighbor's car																				
lumber																				
power mower																				
shorts																				
slacks																				

Vital Stats

Rich, Sandra, Tony, and Ursula each have different ages (13, 15, 16, and 19), heights in centimeters (163, 165, 168, and 175), weights in kilograms (50, 52, 54, and 59), and colors of eyes (blue, green, hazel, and violet). Their last names are Andrews, Blake, Capler, and Drew. Read the clues to find each person's full name, age, height, weight, and eye color.

> Note: Clues which compare ages, heights, and/or weights are talking about the numbers involved, not the units. For example, if a clue says, "The weight of the shortest person is five times that person's age," the clue really means, "The number of kilograms in the weight of the shortest person is the same as five times the number of years in that person's age."

1. The sum of the ages of Capler and Sandra is 1/3 the sum of the weights of Sandra and Tony.

2. The sum of the weights of Tony and Ursula is eight times Tony's age.

3. The sum of the heights of Rich and Andrews is twice the square of Drew's age.

4. Andrews is older than either Capler or Ursula.

5. The person with green eyes is taller than either of the people with violet or hazel eyes.

6. The oldest person is not the tallest.

7. Except for Sandra, the name of the color of each person's eyes has at least one letter other than "E" that is also in the person's name.

8. Tony is taller than Ursula.

9. The shortest person does not have blue eyes.

	Andrews	Blake	Capler	Drew	13	15	16	19	163 cm	165 cm	168 cm	175 cm	50 kg	52 kg	54 kg	59 kg	blue eyes	green eyes	hazel eyes	violet eyes
Rich																				
Sandra																				
Tony																				
Ursula																				
13																				
15																				
16																				
19																				
163 cm																				
165 cm																				
168 cm																				
175 cm																				
50 kg																				
52 kg																				
54 kg																				
59 kg																				
blue eyes																				
green eyes																				
hazel eyes																				
violet eyes																				

All's Fair in Science

Two girls (Victoria and Wanda) and two boys (Yuan-Tung and Zachariah) are working on science fair projects. Their last names are Almont, Bettcher, Corning, and Dowel. Their teachers are Elworth, Fletcher, Garner, and Ignash, and their ages are 9, 10, 11, and 12. One student is studying how the human heart beat changes under different conditions. One is working on magic squares. One is going to enter a rock collection. One is studying how different amounts of sunlight affect the growth of plants. Read the clues to find each person's full name, teacher, age, and project.

1. Fletcher's student is 3/4 as old as Corning.
2. Almont uses a stethoscope for her project.
3. Zachariah is neither the oldest nor the youngest.
4. Wanda is a year older than the girl who is entering the rock collection.
5. Garner's student is not the one doing the sunlight study.
6. Bettcher thinks his project and the project of Ignash's student will both win first prizes.
7. Yuan-Tung is older than Ignash's and Elworth's students.

	Almont	Bettcher	Corning	Dowel	heart	magic squares	rocks	sunlight	Elworth	Fletcher	Garner	Ignash	9	10	11	12
Victoria																
Wanda																
Yuan-Tung																
Zachariah																
heart																
magic squares																
rocks																
sunlight																
Elworth																
Fletcher																
Garner																
Ignash																
9																
10																
11																
12																

Come As You Are

Four couples (Artland, Broad, Crane, and Durkin) were invited to a come-as-you-are party. The wives (Estelle, Faith, Gin-Wei, and Holly) were wearing a muumuu, a police uniform, a robe, and yachting clothes. The husbands (Irwin, James, Kensuke, and Leonardo) were wearing a nurse's uniform, overalls, a suit, and a tuxedo. Read the clues to find each person's full name and the clothes each wore to the party.

1. James is not married to any of these three: Gin-Wei, the woman in the muumuu, or Mrs. Crane.
2. In a game of charades, Estelle and Mrs. Durkin were partners against the man in the suit and Irwin.
3. Mr. Artland and the man in the overalls were born in the same town.
4. The Broads both wore uniforms.
5. Faith is not married to any of these three: James, the man in the suit, or Mr. Artland.
6. Holly lives between the woman in the robe and the man in the tuxedo.
7. The man in the nurse's uniform beat Faith's husband at tennis.
8. Mrs. Crane and the woman in the yachting clothes performed in a comedy skit written by Irwin, Kensuke, and the man in the tuxedo.
9. Holly beat Mrs. Broad at bowling yesterday afternoon.

	Estelle	Faith	Gin-Wei	Holly	muumuu	police uniform	robe	yachting clothes	Irwin	James	Kensuke	Leonardo	nurse's uniform	overalls	suit	tuxedo
Artland																
Broad																
Crane																
Durkin																
muumuu																
police uniform																
robe																
yachting clothes																
Irwin																
James																
Kensuke																
Leonardo																
nurse's uniform																
overalls																
suit																
tuxedo																

All in a Row

Stevens, Taylor, Uhlman, and Wagner, whose first names are Harry, Ivan, Joy, and Karen live in a row of houses (1, 2, 3, and 4). Each of them lives alone in a house painted green, pink, white, or yellow. All four of the people have formed a car pool even though only three people own a car (Chevrolet, Ford, and Oldsmobile). Read the clues to find each person's full name, position in the row of houses, house color, and type of car.

1. Stevens and Ivan are always ready early, while Taylor is always right on time and Joy is always a minute or two late.
2. The man who lives in the second house does not have a car.
3. The owner of the Oldsmobile has her car washed every week, but the owner of the Ford, who lives in the fourth house, thinks this is a waste of money.
4. The yellow house is next door to the pink house.
5. Harry and Karen do not live next door to each other.
6. The green house is not next to either the white house or the yellow house.
7. The owner of the Chevrolet lives in the pink house.
8. Uhlman lives two doors away from the green house.
9. Taylor does not live in the first house.
10. Joy lives next door to Ivan.

	Stevens	Taylor	Uhlman	Wagner	1	2	3	4	green	pink	white	yellow	Chevrolet	Ford	Oldsmobile	none
Harry																
Ivan																
Joy																
Karen																
1																
2																
3																
4																
green																
pink																
white																
yellow																
Chevrolet																
Ford																
Oldsmobile																
none																

Facts on Five

Abby, Bruce, Diane, Joe, and Nancy, whose last names are Baker, Carlyle, Doyle, Eaton, and Horton have nicknames (Curly, Lefty, Nicky, Speedy, and Woody). Each drives a different kind of car (compact, sports car, sedan, station wagon, and van) to work (carpenter, executive, homemaker, salesperson, and secretary). The cars are black, blue, green, red, and yellow. Read the clues to find each person's full name, nickname, occupation, kind of car, and color of car.

1. Nicky, who does not do manual labor, and the secretary priced new cars together.
2. The carpenter, who is not Bruce, bought a car handy both for hauling work tools and for camping trips.
3. Nancy bought a blue car big enough to haul her German Shepherd dog, her four kids, and the weekly groceries for her family of six, all at one time.
4. The executive's car was not the most expensive, but it is the most conservative, both in color and in style.
5. Joe, contrary to his nickname, took Lefty and Horton for a slow ride in the country in his new sports car.
6. The salesperson, on the advice of Eaton, her boss, bought a car that conserves more gas than any of the other styles.
7. The homemaker, who is not Carlyle, did not buy a red or yellow car, and Curly did not buy a blue or green car.
8. Baker likes his yellow car better than Horton's green van.
9. The carpenter once did some work for Nancy.
10. Neither Lefty nor the carpenter knows the salesperson.
11. Nicky didn't buy the green car or the red car.
12. Abby owns the red car.

	Baker	Carlyle	Doyle	Eaton	Horton	Curly	Lefty	Nicky	Speedy	Woody	compact	sports car	sedan	station wagon	van	black	blue	green	red	yellow	carpenter	executive	homemaker	salesperson	secretary
Abby																									
Bruce																									
Diane																									
Joe																									
Nancy																									
Curly																									
Lefty																									
Speedy																									
Nicky																									
Woody																									
compact																									
sports car																									
sedan																									
station wagon																									
van																									
black																									
blue																									
green																									
red																									
yellow																									
carpenter																									
executive																									
homemaker																									
salesperson																									
secretary																									

Father and Child

Five children (Sarah, Tammy, Udall, Vincent, and Walter) and their fathers (Fritz, Gerhard, Homer, Ian, and Jules) live in a row of houses (1, 2, 3, 4, and 5). Each father has only one child and has the same last name as his child (Nelson, Orthman, Pierce, Quinlan, and Roth). Each father has a different occupation (accountant, bricklayer, carpenter, detective, and electrician), and each child is interested in a different occupation (karate teacher, locksmith, mystery writer, X-ray technician, and zookeeper). Read the clues to find each child's full name, occupation of interest, father's first name, occupation, and house position.

1. Homer's and Roth's sons are both straight-A students.
2. Udall lives two doors away from Ian's son and three doors away from Orthman.
3. Pierce's son and the future locksmith live next door to each other.
4. The father of the girl who wants to be a zookeeper and the carpenter, who lives next door, often drive to work together.
5. The boys whose fathers' occupations do not require manual skills live on one end of the row.
6. The carpenter's house is after both Fritz's and the would-be locksmith's houses.
7. Mr. Quinlan and Homer and the carpenter were invited to go over to a party at Walter's house.
8. Nelson and the daughters of Fritz and the electrician were all in the school play.
9. Gerhard's and Quinlan's houses are next door to Udall's house.
10. The girl who wants to be a mystery writer often goes over to the detective's house to talk to him about plots.
11. Sarah lives next door to Homer.
12. The future locksmith's house is before the accountant's house.
13. The future X-ray technician lives two doors away from Pierce.
14. The electrician and the future mystery writer's father belong to the same book club.
15. Walter's last name is not Roth.

	Nelson	Orthman	Pierce	Quinlan	Roth	Fritz	Gerhard	Homer	Ian	Jules	accountant	bricklayer	carpenter	detective	electrician	karate teacher	locksmith	mystery writer	X-ray technician	zookeeper	1	2	3	4	5
Sarah																									
Tammy																									
Udall																									
Vincent																									
Walter																									
Fritz																									
Gerhard																									
Homer																									
Ian																									
Jules																									
accountant																									
bricklayer																									
carpenter																									
detective																									
electrician																									
karate teacher																									
locksmith																									
mystery writer																									
X-ray technician																									
zookeeper																									
1																									
2																									
3																									
4																									
5																									

Teeing Off

Five women whose first names are Portia, Queenie, Ramona, Sherry, and Thelma, and whose last names are Arthur, Barlow, Castor, Dinkman, and Ebber, competed for a $50,000 prize in a golf tournament. Each wears a different color of golf cap (maroon, orange, violet, white, and yellow), and each had a different caddy (Faye, Gwen, Hera, Ina, and Jan). Their scores for the first round were 66, 68, 69, 70, and 71 and tee-off positions (1st, 2nd, 3rd, 4th, and 5th). Read the clues to find each woman's full name, cap color, caddy, score, and tee-off position.

1. Sherry and Barlow and the golfer in the orange cap have met at other tournaments, but neither the golfer who had the lowest score nor Ina's golfer had met any of the others before today.
2. Portia sliced into the rough when she teed off for the first hole, and Ebber, who teed off right after her, followed suit.
3. Queenie and Arthur and the golfer who wears the yellow cap had lunch together yesterday.
4. Castor found out that Hera's golfer, Ramona, and the golfer who teed off first today all practiced putting together yesterday morning.
5. Gwen's golfer, who spent all of yesterday morning studying the course, teed off today before Portia and after the golfer who wears the maroon cap.
6. Faye's golfer beat Queenie by three strokes.
7. The golfer in the violet cap teed off after Dinkman and had a score two strokes worse than the golfer who teed off second today.
8. Jan's golfer did not have the worst score today.

	Arthur	Barlow	Castor	Dinkman	Ebber	Faye	Gwen	Hera	Ina	Jan	maroon	orange	violet	white	yellow	1st	2nd	3rd	4th	5th	66	68	69	70	71
Portia																									
Queenie																									
Ramona																									
Sherry																									
Thelma																									
Faye																									
Gwen																									
Hera																									
Ina																									
Jan																									
maroon																									
orange																									
violet																									
white																									
yellow																									
1st																									
2nd																									
3rd																									
4th																									
5th																									
66																									
68																									
69																									
70																									
71																									

Feelings for Flowers

Six women (Anne, Betty, Carol, Edith, Mary, and Vera) entered flowers (dahlia, lily, orchid, rose, tulip, and violet) in this year's flower show. Each flower won a different prize—grand award, 1st, 2nd, 3rd, honorable mention, and special award, listed in descending order. No woman who entered a flower in last year's show entered the same kind of flower this year, nor did her entry win the same prize as in last year's show. Each woman believes that plants have feelings, and they each give their flowers a special treatment because of this (moving it about, playing music to it, reading it poetry, leaving it in solitude, keeping it in as much sunlight as possible, and talking to it). The last names of the women are Brown, Chorn, Dorman, Felding, Lucas, and Smith. Read the clues to find each woman's full name, flower, special treatment, and prize won this year.

1. Mary, who has always had a green thumb, was talked into entering the show for the first time this year by Mrs. Smith, whose dahlia won an honorable mention award last year.
2. The rose won a higher award than either the tulip or the orchid this year, but it didn't do as well as Vera's entry.
3. Edith raised her prize-winning flower this year in a pot in her apartment, being careful to move the pot each day so that the flower could have various experiences.
4. Betty met Mrs. Felding for the first time at this year's flower show, although both had entered flowers in last year's show.
5. Although Mrs. Dorman has good luck with flowers now, there was a time when she just couldn't seem to get any flower to grow.
6. Mrs. Lucas' entry this year did better than both her entry last year and this year's tulip, and she is going to try for an even better prize next year.
7. Mrs. Brown has never had any luck in growing flowers herself, but she has a superb gardener and so entered one of the many beautiful roses from her garden in the show.
8. This year's grand award winner had poetry read to it every day, but neither the violet nor the lily had been so lucky.
9. Anne plays music to her flowers, but Carol and Mrs. Dorman believe that plants thrive best on the sound of the human voice.
10. Carol's entry this year did all right, but it did not do as well as this year's dahlia or tulip.
11. Vera and Mary agree that leaving a plant in the sun too long tires it out, but the special award winner had been left in the sun as much as possible.
12. The violet was awarded second prize this year, and the orchid's prize was two places below that.

	Brown	Chorn	Dorman	Felding	Lucas	Smith	dahlia	lily	orchid	rose	tulip	violet	moving	music	poetry	solitude	sunlight	talking	grand award	1st	2nd	3rd	honorable mention	special award
Anne																								
Betty																								
Carol																								
Edith																								
Mary																								
Vera																								
dahlia																								
lily																								
orchid																								
rose																								
tulip																								
violet																								
moving																								
music																								
poetry																								
solitude																								
sunlight																								
talking																								
grand award																								
1st																								
2nd																								
3rd																								
honorable mention																								
special award																								

Six Bowlers

Art, Bob, Chuck, Dave, Ed, and Frank, who are a cashier, a firefighter, a manager, a plumber, a police officer, and a public school teacher, each bowled on a different team (Anchors, Framers, Jinxes, Rollers, Scorers, and Toppers) in a bowling league. No man was on the same team as the team he was on last year, nor did his team this year end up in the same position as his team last year. The last names of the men are Miller, Newton, Oliver, Payton, Queen, and Renalt. Read the clues to find each man's full name, occupation, team name, and this year's final position (1st, 2nd, 3rd, 4th, 5th, and 6th).

1. Bob and Oliver bowled together on the Framers last year, which finished in fifth position then, even though Bob has always carried a 190 average.
2. The manager, who was on the first-place team this year, bowled with the Toppers last year and did not bowl with the Anchors this year.
3. Chuck's team ended up below both the Framers and the Scorers.
4. Bob and Frank bowled a practice game with the firefighter, who was on the sixth-place team.
5. Miller, who carried a 185 average last year with the Scorers, bowled on a team this year which finished neither first nor sixth.
6. The Rollers ended in a higher position than either the Scorers or the Jinxes, but not as high as Frank's team.
7. Ed gave Renalt some tips which improved his average by quite a bit this year.
8. Art is a police officer, but neither Chuck nor Queen works for any kind of public body.
9. Dave, the cashier, carries a consistent average which doesn't vary much one way or the other from year to year.
10. The Jinxes ended up in fifth place, two places below the Anchors.
11. Queen's average has improved by 20 points since he started taking a 4-step, instead of a 5-step, approach this year.
12. Newton, whose average has noticeable ups and downs, is on the Rollers this year.

	Miller	Newton	Oliver	Payton	Queen	Renalt	Anchors	Framers	Jinxes	Rollers	Scorers	Toppers	cashier	firefighter	manager	plumber	police officer	school teacher	1st	2nd	3rd	4th	5th	6th
Art																								
Bob																								
Chuck																								
Dave																								
Ed																								
Frank																								
Anchors																								
Framers																								
Jinxes																								
Rollers																								
Scorers																								
Toppers																								
cashier																								
firefighter																								
manager																								
plumber																								
police officer																								
school teacher																								
1st																								
2nd																								
3rd																								
4th																								
5th																								
6th																								

Students of Mathematics

Amy, Brad, Carl, Dorothy, Elaine, and Fred are university students (at MIT, Tulane, UCLA, University of Denver, University of Nebraska, and Wayne State University) who are specializing in mathematics (computer programming, game theory, measure theory, number theory, probability theory, and uses of vector spaces). Their last names are Garrett, Horner, Iwasi, Jackson, King, and Landon. Their home cities are Chicago, Denver, Kansas City, New York City, Phoenix, and Seattle. Read the clues to find each student's full name, mathematics speciality, university, and home city.

1. By plane, no student's home city is within 600 miles of the university he or she attends.
2. Horner, whose home city is not Phoenix and who does not attend the University of Nebraska, once dated Brad, whose home city is Denver.
3. Because of money problems, neither Amy nor the girl from Seattle could attend MIT.
4. Elaine, who specializes in number theory, doesn't know Landon, but she has heard about him from a friend who has classes with him at MIT.
5. The game theorist, who is from Seattle, and King write to each other.
6. Carl specializes in probability theory, but Fred and Jackson specialize in applied, rather than theoretical, mathematics.
7. Fred's grades are better than the Wayne State University and University of Nebraska students' grades, but they aren't as good as the Chicago student's grades.
8. The student from New York City specializes in computer programming and transferred from the University of Denver to a school closer to her home.
9. The UCLA student's home is east of the Tulane student's home and west of the MIT student's home.
10. King told Brad that she'd like to meet Iwasi, who attends Tulane.
11. Neither King nor Horner attends Wayne State University.

	Garrett	Horner	Iwasi	Jackson	King	Landon	computer programming	game theory	measure theory	number theory	probability theory	vector spaces	MIT	Tulane	UCLA	University of Denver	University of Nebraska	Wayne State University	Chicago	Denver	Kansas City	New York City	Phoenix	Seattle
Amy																								
Brad																								
Carl																								
Dorothy																								
Elaine																								
Fred																								
computer programming																								
game theory																								
measure theory																								
number theory																								
probability theory																								
vector spaces																								
MIT																								
Tulane																								
UCLA																								
University of Denver																								
University of Nebraska																								
Wayne State University																								
Chicago																								
Denver																								
Kansas City																								
New York City																								
Phoenix																								
Seattle																								

Horsing Around

Six horses (Apollo, Beauty, Charmer, Dazzler, Enchanter, and Fascinator) were ridden in a race today by jockeys Geyer, Harmon, Ivers, Jason, Klinger, and Lehman. Their trainers are Manning, Newman, Oster, Pauling, Quell, and Raymond. Their owners are Sampson, Tuller, Ulrich, Viner, Werner, and Yolder. The last previous tracks the horses raced were Arlington, Belmont, Churchill Downs, Hialeah, Pimlico, and Santa Anita, each horse racing at a different track. The horses' colors are amber, black, chestnut, gray, tan, and white. Read the clues to find each horse's name, jockey, trainer, owner, racetrack, color, and position in today's race.

1. Beauty came in ahead of the horse trained by Newman but behind Tuller's horse.
2. Charmer, the black horse, and the horse that came in fourth sometimes all work out together.
3. Pauling, the jockey for her horse, and Jason, Geyer, and Apollo's jockey all went bowling two days ago.
4. The horse that last raced at Churchill Downs came in ahead of the chestnut horse but behind the horse trained by Newman.
5. Dazzler's owner refused to sell him to Werner and Ulrich even though they offered him a fair price for the horse.
6. The tan horse came in ahead of both Tuller's horse, which did not last race at Belmont, and the horse that last raced at Hialeah.
7. Oster and the trainers of Enchanter and Werner's horse and the gray horse talked about pooling their monies to buy a horse of their own.
8. Apollo, Beauty, and Charmer are all temperamental, but the horses ridden by Harmon, Ivers, and Lehman are easy to handle.
9. Yolder, Viner, and Sampson belong to the same sorority.
10. The amber horse came in ahead of both the white and the gray horses but behind the black horse.
11. Ulrich told Fascinator's owner that he thought the horse that last raced at Hialeah is handsomer than either of theirs but not as dependable as theirs or as the horse Manning trained.
12. Werner and the owners of Apollo, Beauty, and Fascinator compared diets. Werner said he wanted to lose some weight, but the others all said they wanted to gain some.
13. The owner of the horse ridden by Klinger said he is going to discharge the trainer and try to get either Newman or Enchanter's trainer.
14. Neither Viner's horse, nor Yolder's horse, nor the horse that last raced at Hialeah finished last today.
15. The horses that finished first and last today are both hard to handle.
16. The horse ridden by Jason did not finish last today.
17. Geyer said the owner of the horse he rode today told him she was pleased with the way the horse was handled today and that both he and the trainer, who is not Quell or Raymond, are to get bonuses.
18. Viner's horse, which has never been ridden by Harmon, raced last at Pimlico.
19. The horse trained by Quell, which is not Apollo, has never raced at Belmont or Santa Anita.
20. The owner of the horse Ivers rode today said he is planning a vacation with his family.
21. Yolder would like to hire either Quell or Manning, but both prefer to work with the horses they're already training.
22. The horse Manning trains is not tan.

	Geyer	Harmon	Ivers	Jason	Klinger	Lehman	Manning	Newman	Oster	Pauling	Quell	Raymond	Sampson	Tuller	Ulrich	Viner	Werner	Yolder	Arlington	Belmont	Churchill Downs	Hialeah	Pimlico	Santa Anita	amber	black	chestnut	gray	tan	white	1st	2nd	3rd	4th	5th	6th
Apollo																																				
Beauty																																				
Charmer																																				
Dazzler																																				
Enchanter																																				
Fascinator																																				
Manning																																				
Newman																																				
Oster																																				
Pauling																																				
Quell																																				
Raymond																																				
Sampson																																				
Tuller																																				
Ulrich																																				
Viner																																				
Werner																																				
Yolder																																				
Arlington																																				
Belmont																																				
Churchill Downs																																				
Hialeah																																				
Pimlico																																				
Santa Anita																																				
amber																																				
black																																				
chestnut																																				
gray																																				
tan																																				
white																																				
1st																																				
2nd																																				
3rd																																				
4th																																				
5th																																				
6th																																				

Three and Three

Three females (Chi-Wei, Elseyn, and Francesca) and three males (Arturo, Bernardo, and Dominic) are of different ages (13, 16, 17, 19, 20, and 25), weights (in kg—48, 50, 56, 59, 77, and 82) and heights (in cm—155, 163, 167, 168, 182, and 187). Each was born in a different month (April, May, June, July, August, and November) and on a different day of the month (3rd, 4th, 10th, 11th, 12th, and 22nd). Their last names are Guernari, Houh, Ito, Juarez, Kung, and Lee. Read the clues to find each person's full name and vital statistics: age, weight, height, and month and day born. Some clues refer to a month by its number (2 is February, for example).

1. All of Arturo's vital statistics are prime numbers.
2. The youngest person is not the tallest.
3. All of Kung's vital statistics are multiples of 4.
4. Except for his age, all of Dominic's vital statistics are multiples of 11.
5. Except for the month of birth, all of Houh's vital statistics are multiples of 5.
6. Francesca's weight is a multiple of her age, and the same is true of Houh's weight and age. (Francesca is not Houh.)
7. Chi-Wei's age and month of birth are both perfect squares.
8. Lee's birth month is not a prime number, and neither is Elseyn's.
9. Except for his age, Bernardo's vital statistics are all even numbers.
10. Ito is older than Juarez but younger than Guernari, who is younger than Lee.
11. Juarez is taller than Ito.
12. The youngest person was born in an earlier month than the person who was born on the third of the month.
13. Elseyn's age is a multiple of the day of the month on which she was born.

	Guernari	Houh	Ito	Juarez	Kung	Lee	13	16	17	19	20	25	48 kg	50 kg	56 kg	59 kg	77 kg	82 kg	155 cm	163 cm	167 cm	168 cm	182 cm	187 cm	April	May	June	July	August	November	3rd	4th	10th	11th	12th	22nd
Arturo																																				
Bernardo																																				
Chi-Wei																																				
Dominic																																				
Elseyn																																				
Francesca																																				
13																																				
16																																				
17																																				
19																																				
20																																				
25																																				
48 kg																																				
50 kg																																				
56 kg																																				
59 kg																																				
77 kg																																				
82 kg																																				
155 cm																																				
163 cm																																				
167 cm																																				
168 cm																																				
182 cm																																				
187 cm																																				
April																																				
May																																				
June																																				
July																																				
August																																				
November																																				
3rd																																				
4th																																				
10th																																				
11th																																				
12th																																				
22nd																																				

Nine Singles

Nine men on a big league baseball team joined the team at different times (1st - 9th). Their first names are José, Kevin, Lou, Mike, Neil, Otis, Paul, Quincy, and Rick. Their last names are Abbott, Baker, Carter, Drake, Edwards, Fraser, Grant, Horner, and Irving. Their positions are 1st base, 2nd base, 3rd base, shortstop, left field, center field, right field, pitcher, and catcher. Their ages are 21, 22, 23, 25, 26, 27, 28, 33, and 34. Read the clues to find each man's full name, position, age, order he joined the team, and marital status (single men have no children and have never been married).

1. Otis has an ERA of 3.27 so far this year.
2. The left fielder, Carter, and Kevin were the last three to join the team.
3. The catcher, Drake, and Rick were the first three to join the team.
4. The shortstop is 3/4 as old as the first baseman.
5. Horner, Neil, and Lou go bowling together.
6. Kevin and the third baseman sometimes go on double dates together.
7. Carter's mother is dating Neil.
8. The age of the fifth man to join the team is 1/3 as much as twice the age of the catcher.
9. The first man to join the team is 7 years older than the 4th man to join the team and is 5 years older than Quincy.
10. The catcher joined the team before the first baseman.
11. Paul's sister is married to Edwards.
12. Horner, Drake, Lou, José, and their wives went golfing last week.
13. Otis, Quincy, and Abbott took their kids to the zoo yesterday.
14. One infielder, two outfielders, and one other player are married. The other players are single.
15. Irving suggested to Mike and Rick the joke they pulled on Grant and Baker, and then Lou and Edwards pulled it on him a couple of days later.
16. Irving is older than Kevin but younger than Baker.
17. The third baseman is the oldest of the infielders, and Irving is the oldest of the outfielders.
18. The sixth man to join the team is older than Irving and younger than Neil.
19. Paul's age is the average of Horner's and the left fielder's ages.
20. Kevin, Rick, and the shortstop collided last week when they all ran to catch the same ball.
21. The center fielder is younger than the right fielder.
22. Abbott joined the team after Mike but before Grant.
23. The third man to join the team is older than the second man to join.

	Abbott	Baker	Carter	Drake	Edwards	Fraser	Grant	Horner	Irving	1st base	2nd base	3rd base	shortstop	left field	center field	right field	pitcher	catcher	21	22	23	25	26	27	28	33	34	1st	2nd	3rd	4th	5th	6th	7th	8th	9th
José																																				
Kevin																																				
Lou																																				
Mike																																				
Neil																																				
Otis																																				
Paul																																				
Quincy																																				
Rick																																				
1st base																																				
2nd base																																				
3rd base																																				
shortstop																																				
left field																																				
center field																																				
right field																																				
pitcher																																				
catcher																																				
21																																				
22																																				
23																																				
25																																				
26																																				
27																																				
28																																				
33																																				
34																																				
1st																																				
2nd																																				
3rd																																				
4th																																				
5th																																				
6th																																				
7th																																				
8th																																				
9th																																				

Name	Married/Single
Abbott	
Baker	
Carter	
Drake	
Edwards	
Fraser	
Grant	
Horner	
Irving	

Costume Party

Five married couples (Uster, Vincent, Wyler, Yang, and Zorbet) went to a costume party. The women (Anita, Beth, Cornelia, Driselda, and Esther) dressed as Cinderella, Gretel, Queen of Sheba, Sleeping Beauty, and Snow White. The men (Gerhard, Isaac, Len, Reuben, and Terrance) dressed as Frankenstein, Hansel, Moses, Napoleon, and Prince Charming. The streets where the couples live are Cedar, Chestnut, Elm, Maple, and Redwood. Read the clues to find each person's full name, costume, and street. Do not count "y" as a vowel in any of the clues.

1. There is exactly one common vowel in:
   a. each couple's last name and the wife's first name.
   b. each couple's last name and the husband's first name.
   c. each man's first name and his wife's first name, except for the Zorbets and Yangs.
   d. each couple's street name and the husband's first name.
   e. each couple's street name and the wife's first name.
   f. each couple's street name and their last name.
2. There is at least one common vowel in:
   a. each man's costume name and his first name.
   b. each woman's costume name and her first name.
   c. each woman's costume name and her last name.
3. For the couples who live on Maple and Cedar, both vowels in each couple's street name are found in both the husband's and the wife's costume names.
4. The vowels in the street name of the Vincents are both found in the wife's costume name, but only one of the vowels is in the husband's costume name.
5. The Zorbets' street name has two vowels, but only the "E" is in the wife's costume name.
6. The Usters were the only couple both dressed as fairy tale characters.
7. The Queen of Sheba is not married to Hansel.
8. Len, Napoleon, and Driselda's husband all had to be talked into going to the party, but they had a good time after they got there.
9. Moses' wife and Cornelia both made their own costumes.
10. Esther and Mrs. Uster both bought their costumes.
11. Isaac does not live on Cedar.
12. Sleeping Beauty is not married to Len.
13. Esther's husband, Terrance, and Frankenstein all work at the same place.
14. Reuben's wife is not Gretel.
15. Frankenstein does not live on Elm.

	Uster	Vincent	Wyler	Yang	Zorbet	Gerhard	Isaac	Len	Reuben	Terrance	Cinderella	Gretel	Queen of Sheba	Sleeping Beauty	Snow White	Frankenstein	Hansel	Moses	Napoleon	Prince Charming	Cedar	Chestnut	Elm	Maple	Redwood
Anita																									
Beth																									
Cornelia																									
Driselda																									
Esther																									
Gerhard																									
Isaac																									
Len																									
Reuben																									
Terrance																									
Cinderella																									
Gretel																									
Queen of Sheba																									
Sleeping Beauty																									
Snow White																									
Frankenstein																									
Hansel																									
Moses																									
Napoleon																									
Prince Charming																									
Cedar																									
Chestnut																									
Elm																									
Maple																									
Redwood																									

Party Time

Five couples (Aston, Barler, Cauchy, Dick, and Eggler) get together five times a year (Halloween, Independence Day, New Year's Eve, St. Patrick's Day, and Valentine's Day) for a party. Each couple hosts one of the parties at their home (on Palmer, Quinton, Rawlins, Stoddard, and Talbot) and serves a different drink (coffee, fruit juice, iced tea, lemonade, and punch). The wives' first names are Freda, Ginny, Helene, Ilene, and Julia. The husbands' first names are Kermit, Leon, Morton, Norbert, and Orville. The party decorations, food, and costumes are appropriate for each party. Read the clues to find each person's full name, holiday hosted, street, and drink.

1. Mrs. Barler, Julia, and Ilene all shop at the same supermarket.
2. Everyone dressed in green for the party on Quinton.
3. Norbert and his wife picked up the Egglers and the couple who serves lemonade on their way to the Astons' party.
4. Helene and Freda both asked Mrs. Dick for the recipe for the frosting on the heart-shaped cake she served at her party.
5. The couple on Stoddard decorated with pumpkins and served iced tea at their party.
6. Orville told Mr. Eggler he should color the drink green at the Egglers' party, but Mr. Eggler says his wife thinks it will look unappetizing.
7. Ginny's husband made the coffee for their party while Ginny was on the phone with Mrs. Cauchy.
8. Leon, Norbert, and Mr. Barler are all on the school board.
9. The couple on Palmer always look forward to going to the New Year's Eve and Independence Day parties because they like to make noise and stay up late.
10. Orville and his wife had a hard time finding confetti and noisemakers for their last party because they waited too long to go shopping.
11. The Rawlins couple were thinking of moving out of the city, but Orville and the Barlers talked them out of it.
12. Neither Helene nor Kermit lives on Stoddard.
13. The St. Patrick's Day party is not held at either of Kermit's or Helene's houses.
14. The Cauchys and the couple on Talbot sometimes have dinner together at a restaurant.
15. Helene does not live on Rawlins, and neither does Ilene.
16. Ginny is not married to Leon.
17. Fruit juice is not served at Orville's party.

	Freda	Ginny	Helene	Ilene	Julia	Kermit	Leon	Morton	Norbert	Orville	Palmer	Quinton	Rawlins	Stoddard	Talbot	Halloween	Independence Day	New Year's Eve	St. Patrick's Day	Valentine's Day	coffee	fruit juice	iced tea	lemonade	punch
Aston																									
Barler																									
Cauchy																									
Dick																									
Eggler																									
Kermit																									
Leon																									
Morton																									
Norbert																									
Orville																									
Palmer																									
Quinton																									
Rawlins																									
Stoddard																									
Talbot																									
Halloween																									
Independence Day																									
New Year's Eve																									
St. Patrick's Day																									
Valentine's Day																									
coffee																									
fruit juice																									
iced tea																									
lemonade																									
punch																									

Five Families

Following is some information about five families (Allan, Boncher, Crachy, Dorkea, and Effer) who live in different cities (Ulrich, Valley, Willie, Yellow, and Zebra) and states (Alabama, Idaho, Kansas, Ohio, and Tennessee). The fathers' first names are Porter, Quentin, Reuben, Stuart, and Todd. The mothers' first names are Kitty, Leah, Marla, Neva, and Olive. Taking just one child from each family, the children's first names are Frank, Gerald, Helga, Iris, and Julie. Read the clues to find each person's full name, city, and state. A clue which uses only a last name (without "Mr." or "Mrs.") refers to a child.

1. No family lives in a state whose name begins with the same first letter as any member's name (either first or last).
2. No family lives in a city or in a state whose name ends with the same letter as any member's name (either first or last).
3. Not counting duplications, the name of each city has exactly one letter in common with the name of the state in which it is located.
4. Kitty does not live in Willie.
5. The Zebra family visits both the Idaho family and the Dorkea family.
6. Reuben, Frank's father, Mr. Effer, and the man who lives in Tennessee were friends in school.
7. Porter is the godfather of both Allan and Iris.
8. Leah and Mrs. Allan are Stuart's sisters.
9. Except for Todd and Iris, the name of the city where each family lives has at least one letter in common with both names (first and last) of each family member.
10. Nobody in Olive's family knows anyone in any of the other four families.
11. Crachy told his father he wishes they could move out of the midwestern state where they live.
12. Reuben's wife's name has a letter in common with the name of their state.
13. Marla does not have any daughters.
14. Helga's mother is an only child, and so are she and her father.
15. Todd is not married to Olive.
16. When Mr. Dorkea went to visit the Kansas family, he took their twins and his own two children camping.

	Frank	Gerald	Helga	Iris	Julie	Kitty	Leah	Marla	Neva	Olive	Porter	Quentin	Reuben	Stuart	Todd	Ulrich	Valley	Willie	Yellow	Zebra	Alabama	Idaho	Kansas	Ohio	Tennessee
Allan																									
Boncher																									
Crachy																									
Dorkea																									
Effer																									
Kitty																									
Leah																									
Marla																									
Neva																									
Olive																									
Porter																									
Quentin																									
Reuben																									
Stuart																									
Todd																									
Ulrich																									
Valley																									
Willie																									
Yellow																									
Zebra																									
Alabama																									
Idaho																									
Kansas																									
Ohio																									
Tennessee																									

DETAILED SOLUTIONS

Pg. 4-5

NAME	AGE	PET	HOUSE
Ed	11	dog	frame
Marie	9	parakeet	aluminum siding
Natalie	10	cat	brick
Quentin	13	gerbil	stucco

The 11-year-old is not Marie or Natalie (7) or Quentin (4), so he is Ed. The owner of the cat is not 9 or 13 (9) or 11 (1, Ed), so he or she is 10. Then Marie is 9 (9). The cat is owned by a girl (8) but not by Marie (9), so Natalie owns the cat. Then Quentin is 13. The parakeet is owned by a girl (5), so Marie has the parakeet. The girls are 9 and 10, so the dog owner has to be 11 (3), and Marie, 9 years old, lives in the house with aluminum siding (3). Quentin is left to own the gerbil. Then Quentin lives next door to Marie (2), so he doesn't live in the brick house (6, Marie is 9 years old) or the frame house (4), so he lives in the stucco house. Ed, 11 years old, lives a block away from Quentin (4), who lives next door to Marie (2), so Ed doesn't live in the brick house (6). Then Natalie lives in the brick house, and Ed lives in the frame house.

Pg. 6-7

FIRST NAME	LAST NAME	FAVORITE FOOD	STATE	FAVORITE COLOR
Ada	Hill	kidney beans	Pennsylvania	umber
Brian	Farmer	lemon pie	Oregon	red
Carmella	Grey	Idaho potatoes	Nebraska	tan
Daniel	Eaton	jam	Maine	salmon

Hill is female (6) but isn't Carmella (2), so she is Ada. Her favorite color isn't red, salmon, or tan (6), so it is umber. She doesn't live in Nebraska or Oregon (1) or Maine (4, male), so she lives in Pennsylvania. The man (4) who lives in Maine isn't Brian (4), so he is Daniel, and his last name is Eaton (1). His favorite color isn't red (7, 8) or tan (3), so it is salmon. Carmella's favorite color isn't red (7), so it is tan, and Brian's is red. Then Carmella isn't Farmer (3, tan), so Brian is, and Carmella is Grey. Brian doesn't live in Nebraska (5, red), so Carmella does, and so Brian lives in Oregon. The lemon pie eater is Brian (7, red). Carmella's favorite food isn't jam (2) or kidney beans (9, Nebraska), so it is Idaho potatoes. Ada Hill isn't the jam eater (2), so Daniel is, and so Ada's favorite food is kidney beans.

Pg. 8-9

ANIMAL	COLOR	PATTERN	NAME	AGE	ORIGIN
cat	rust	polka-dotted	King	3	Australia
dog	purple	striped	Princess	1	Africa
elephant	red	plaid	Fido	20	India
tiger	green	checkered	Tiny	6	Europe

The ages of the tiger, Fido, and the African animal are 1, 6, and 20 (5), and the ages of the elephant and the African animal are 1 and 20 (1). So we have four descriptions of animals (tiger, Fido, African, elephant) but only three ages, so one of the descriptions is a duplication. The African animal is included in both clues 1 and 5, so none of the other three descriptions is a duplication of this one. Then we are left with three descriptions for two animals—tiger, Fido, and elephant. The tiger isn't Fido (5) or the elephant, so Fido is the elephant. Then the ages of the tiger, the elephant (Fido) and the African animal are 1, 6, and 20 (5), while the ages of the elephant and the African animal are 1 and 20 (1). So the tiger's age is 6, and the tiger is green (2). The cat's age is not 1 or 6 (4) or 20 (3), so it is 3, and its name is King (2). The purple animal and the checkered animal are 1 and 6 (3). The purple animal is not 6 (green tiger), so it is 1, and the checkered animal is 6. Tiny and the striped animal are 1 and 6 (6). The striped animal is not 6 (checkered), so Tiny is 6, and the striped animal is 1. This leaves Princess to be the dog's name. The cat's pattern is not striped (age 1) or plaid (4), so it is polka-dotted. The ages of Fido, the rust-colored animal, and the European animal are 3, 6, and 20 (7). The 6-year-old is not Fido (Tiny) or rust-colored (green), so it is the European animal. Fido, who is the elephant, is not 3 (cat), so Fido is 20, and the rust-colored animal is 3. Then Princess, the dog, is 1 year old, and the elephant is red plaid. The African animal is 1 year old (1, elephant is 20). The cat is not from India (8, polka-dotted), so it is from Australia, and the elephant is from India.

Pg. 10-11

NAME	GRADE	ILLNESS	TEACHER	BEST SUBJECT
Andrea Farrell	4	measles	Mr. Kay	music
Barry Ewell	1	chicken pox	Ms. Jones	reading
Charlene Hunter	2	mumps	Mr. Lorry	arithmetic
Darrell Gorton	5	flu	Ms. Ilger	spelling

Farrell and Gorton are in grades 4 and 5 (2), so Ewell and Hunter are in grades 1 and 2. Ewell is not in grade 2 (5), so he is in grade 1, and so Hunter is in grade 2. Barry is in grade 1 (6), so he is Ewell. Then Gorton, a boy (2), is Darrell, and he had the flu and is in the 5th grade (6). Then Farrell had the measles and is in the 4th grade (2). Darrell's best subject is spelling (8). Music, not the best subject of Barry or Charlene (4), is the best subject of Andrea. Mr. Kay (5) does not teach grade 1 (1, Barry) or grade 5 (1, Darrell) or grade 2 (5), so he teaches grade 4, which makes him Farrell's teacher. Ewell and Gorton are boys, so Hunter and Farrell are girls. Then Hunter, in the 2nd grade, does not have Ms. Jones (3) for a teacher (1), so Ms. Jones is Barry's teacher (3), and Hunter's best subject is arithmetic (2). Then Andrea is not Hunter (music), so Charlene is Hunter, and Andrea is Farrell. All best subjects and students are now paired except reading and Barry, so Barry's best subject is reading. Lorry's student is not Darrell (7, flu), so Charlene is the student, which makes Lorry a man (1). Then Ilger is Darrell's teacher and is a woman (1). Charlene had mumps (7, Lorry), so Barry had chicken pox.

Pg. 12-13

NAME	PROFESSION	NAME OF PROFESSIONAL	TIME
Ardith Ippman	physician	Manning	11:00
Brady Humphrey	dentist	Roberts	9:30
Celeste Frampton	lawyer	Jackson	9:00
Ethan Gardner	veterinarian	Norton	10:00

Ippman's appointment was with the physician (5). Frampton, a woman (1), is not Ardith (1, 2), so she is Celeste. Ippman, the other woman (5), is Ardith. Norton was not seen by Ardith or Brady (2) or Celeste (1, 2, Frampton), so Norton was seen by Ethan. All titles except the lawyer's would be "Dr.," not "Mr." or "Ms.," so Ms. Jackson is the lawyer (4). Her client was not Ardith (physician), Brady (8), or Ethan (Norton), so her client was Celeste. Ardith had the appointment with the physician, so the physician's name is not Norton (Ethan). It is not Roberts (6), so it is Manning. Then Brady saw Roberts. The appointment with Manning was one of the last two (3), so Ippman's appointment was not at 9:00. Neither was Humphrey's (4) or Gardner's (3), so Frampton's appointment was at 9:00. The 9:30 appointment was not Ardith's (3, Manning) or Ethan's (7), so it was Brady's. Brady and Ethan are Gardner and Humphrey. Gardner's appointment is after the appointment with the dentist (3). Since Brady's 9:30 appointment is only the second appointment and the only other appointment so far was the lawyer, Brady is not Gardner (3), so Ethan is, and Brady is Humphrey. Then Humphrey saw the dentist, and Gardner saw the veterinarian. Gardner's appointment was before the one with Manning, so Gardner's appointment was at 10:00, and the appointment with Manning was at 11:00.

Pg. 14-15

LAST NAME	HUSBAND	HUSBAND'S OCCUPATION	WIFE	WIFE'S OCCUPATION
Idwell	Cary	upholsterer	Felicia	osteopath
Jacobs	Derek	secretary	Heather	mathematician
Kroman	Aston	truck driver	Edwina	professor
Lawton	Basil	roofer	Genevieve	nurse

Heather is not the osteopath or the professor (7) or the nurse (2, 6), so she is the mathematician. Edwina is not the nurse (2) or the osteopath (2, 6), so she is the professor. Felicia is not the nurse (1), so she is the osteopath. Then Genevieve is the nurse. The secretary is not Idwell (6), Kroman (3), or Lawton (2, 6), so he is Jacobs. The truck driver is not Idwell (2, 6) or Lawton (2), so he is Kroman. Heather (the mathematician) is not Idwell (5), Kroman (2, truck driver), or Lawton (2), so she is Jacobs. The roofer is not married to the osteopath or the professor (7), so he is married to the nurse, Genevieve. Then, since he isn't the truck driver, he is Lawton (2), so the truck driver (Kroman) is married to Edwina (2). This leaves Felicia to be Mrs. Idwell, and it leaves Mr. Idwell to be the upholsterer. Edwina Kroman's husband isn't Derek (4, professor), Cary (3), or Basil (8), so he is Aston. Heather Jacob's husband, the secretary, isn't Basil (5) or Cary (3), so he is Derek. Basil isn't Idwell (5), so he is Lawton, and Cary is Idwell.

Pg. 16-17

NAME	PLACE	DISTANCE	TRANSPORT	ITEM
Arthur Gaucher	group of stores	3 miles	jogged	shorts
Bertha Eggleston	shopping mall	5 miles	neighbor's car	power mower
Carlo Hinnel	local store	1 block	family car	lumber
Donna Friar	downtown	10 miles	bus	slacks

Combining clues 3 and 4, we find that the lumber was purchased 1 block away, the jogger went 3 miles, the shopping mall is 5 miles away, and the slacks were purchased 10 miles away. A woman took the bus downtown (5), but she wasn't Bertha (5), so she was Donna. The only distance which is half of another distance is 5 miles, so Bertha went 5 miles and Donna went 10 miles (5). Then Donna bought the slacks, and Bertha went to the shopping mall. Eggleston, a woman (1), went in a neighbor's car (1). She isn't Donna (bus), so Eggleston is Bertha. She bought either the lumber or the power mower (1) but not the lumber (4, man), so Bertha bought the power mower. Donna, who went farther than Bertha, isn't Hinnel (5), so Hinnel is a man, and Gaucher is the other man (2). Then Donna is Friar. Carlo didn't buy the shorts (6), so Arthur did, and Carlo bought the lumber. Gaucher didn't buy the lumber (2), so he bought the shorts. Then Gaucher is Arthur, and Hinnel is Carlo. Gaucher didn't go to the local store (2), so Hinnel did, and Gaucher went to the group of stores. Carlo isn't the jogger (4, lumber), so he took the family car, and Arthur jogged.

Pg. 18-19

NAME	AGE	HEIGHT (cm)	WEIGHT (kg)	EYES
Rich Capler	15	175	59	blue
Sandra Andrews	19	163	52	violet
Tony Drew	13	168	50	green
Ursula Blake	16	165	54	hazel

Eight times the ages are 104, 120, 128, and 152. There are no two weights whose sum is 120, 128, or 152, so Tony's age is 13 (2). The only two weights whose sum is 104 are 50 and 54, so Tony's and Ursula's weights are 50 and 54. The squares of the ages are 169, 225, 256, and 361. Twice these are 338, 450, 512, and 722. The only two heights which total any of these are 163 and 175 (total = 338), so Drew's age is 13 (3) (and so Drew is Tony), and the heights of Rich and Andrews are 163 and 175. Capler is not Sandra (1) or Ursula (4), so he is Rich. Andrews is not Ursula (4), so she is Sandra. Then Ursula is Blake. Tony Drew is 13, and Sandra Andrews is older than either of the remaining two people (4), so Sandra is 19. Then Sandra Andrews is not the tallest (6), so her height is 163 cm, which makes Rich's height 175 cm. Tony is taller than Ursula (8), so Tony's height is 168 cm, and Ursula's is 165 cm. Sandra Andrews' eyes are not blue (9), green (5), or hazel (7, Sandra is the exception), so they are violet. Tony Drew doesn't have blue or hazel eyes (7), so his eyes are green. Rich Capler doesn't have hazel eyes (5, Rich is the tallest), so his eyes are blue, and Ursula's eyes are hazel. The sum of the ages of Rich Capler (15 or 16) and Sandra Andrews (19) is 34 or 35. Three times this is 102 or 105, so this is the sum of the weights of Sandra Andrews (52 or 59) and Tony Drew (50 or 54) (1). With these restrictions imposed, Sandra's weight has to be 52 and Tony's has to be 50, thus forcing Ursula's weight to be 54 and Rich's to be 59. Also, the sum of Sandra's and Tony's weights, 102, makes Rich Capler's age 15 (1), so Ursula is 16.

Pg. 20-21

NAME	PROJECT	TEAM	AGE
Victoria Dowel	rock collection	Fletcher	9
Wanda Almont	human heartbeat	Ignash	10
Yuan-Tung Corning	magic squares	Garner	12
Zachariah Bettcher	sunlight and plants	Elworth	11

Wanda is not the girl entering the rock collection (4), so Victoria is. Almont, a girl (2), is doing the heart study (2), so she is Wanda. Neither Zachariah (3) nor Yuan-Tung (7) is the youngest, so Victoria (4, rock collection) is the youngest, 9, and Wanda is 10 (4). Then Zachariah, who is not the oldest (3), is 11, and Yuan-Tung is 12. Fletcher's student is 9 and Corning is 12 (1), so Victoria is Fletcher's student and Yuan-Tung is Corning. The other boy is Bettcher (6), so he is Zachariah. By elimination, Victoria is Dowel. Yuan-Tung is not the student of Ignash or Elworth (7), so he is Garner's student. He is not doing the sunlight study (5, Garner), so he is working on magic squares, and Zachariah is doing the sunlight study. Zachariah is not Ignash's student (6, Bettcher), so he is Elworth's student, and Wanda is Ignash's student.

Pg. 22-23

LAST NAME	WIFE	WIFE'S CLOTHING	HUSBAND	HUSBAND'S CLOTHING
Artland	Gin-Wei	yachting clothes	Leonardo	tuxedo
Broad	Estelle	police uniform	James	nurse's uniform
Crane	Faith	robe	Irwin	overalls
Durkin	Holly	muumuu	Kensuke	suit

Mrs. Broad wore a police uniform and Mr. Broad wore a nurse's uniform (4). Mrs. Crane didn't wear a muumuu (1) or yachting clothes (8), so she wore a robe. Mr. Artland didn't wear overalls (3) or a suit (5), so he wore a tuxedo. He isn't Irwin or Kensuke (8, tuxedo) or James (5), so he is Leonardo. Faith's husband didn't wear a tuxedo (5, Artland), a suit (5), or a nurse's uniform (7), so he wore overalls. The suit wasn't worn by Irwin (2) or James (5), so it was worn by Kensuke. Holly's husband didn't wear a nurse's uniform (9, Broad) or a tuxedo (6), so he wore a suit. Then Holly is married to Kensuke. James isn't the husband of Faith (5) or Gin-Wei (1), so he is married to Estelle. Then James didn't wear overalls (Faith's husband), so he wore the nurse's uniform. So James and Estelle are the Broads. The clothes of all husbands except Gin-Wei's are accounted for, so Gin-Wei is married to the tuxedo wearer, Leonardo Artland. Gin-Wei did not wear the muumuu (1), so she wore the yachting clothes. Then Mrs. Durkin wore the muumuu. Holly didn't wear the robe (6), so Faith did, and Holly wore the muumuu. Then Faith is Mrs. Crane, and Holly is Mrs. Durkin. The only man left, Irwin, is Mr. Crane.

Pg. 24-25

NAME	HOUSE	POSITION	CAR
Harry Taylor	green	4	Ford
Ivan Uhlman	yellow	2	none
Joy Wagner	pink	3	Chevrolet
Karen Stevens	white	1	Oldsmobile

From clues 4 and 6, the order of the houses is either W, Y, P, G, or G, P, Y, W. The man in the second house doesn't have a car (2), and the owner of the Chevrolet lives in the pink house (7), so the order is not G, P, Y, W. Then the order is W, Y, P, G, with no car for the yellow house, the Chevrolet for the pink house, and the Ford for the green house (3, fourth house), which leaves the Oldsmobile for the white house. A woman lives in the first house (3, Oldsmobile), and a man lives in the second house (2). If the order is woman, man, man, woman, then clue 10 gives us either Joy, Ivan, Harry, Karen, or Karen, Harry, Ivan, Joy, both of which contradict clue 5. Therefore, the order is woman, man, woman, man. Uhlman lives in the second house (8). From clue 1, Uhlman is either Ivan or Joy, but a man lives in the second house, so Uhlman is Ivan. Karen cannot be in the third house, for this would put Harry in the fourth house, contradicting clue 5. So Karen is in the first house, Joy is in the third, and Harry is in the fourth. Since Ivan is Uhlman, Joy is Wagner (1). Taylor is not in the first house (9), so Karen is Stevens, and Harry is Taylor.

Pg. 26-27

NAME	NICKNAME	CAR	CAR COLOR	OCCUPATION
Abby Carlyle	Curly	compact	red	salesperson
Bruce Eaton	Nicky	sedan	black	executive
Diane Horton	Woody	van	green	carpenter
Joe Baker	Speedy	sports car	yellow	secretary
Nancy Doyle	Lefty	station wagon	blue	homemaker

The salesperson bought the compact car (6). Joe's nickname is Speedy (5), and he bought the sports car (5). Nancy bought a blue car (3), Abby bought a red one (12), the executive bought a black sedan (4), and Horton bought a green van (8). Then Joe's sports car is not black (sedan), blue (Nancy), green (van), or red (Abby), so it is yellow, and so Joe is Baker (8). The carpenter didn't buy the sports car (2), so Joe is not the carpenter. Neither is he the executive (black car), the homemaker (7), nor the salesperson (compact car). So Joe is the secretary. Horton, who has the green van, is not Curly (7), Lefty (5), or Nicky (11), so Horton is Woody. Nancy doesn't have the compact (3), the sedan (black), or the van (green), so she has the station wagon. She is not the carpenter (9), the executive (sedan), or the salesperson (compact), so she is the homemaker. Bruce is not the carpenter (2) or the salesperson (6, female), so he is the executive, who has the black sedan. Then Diane owns the green car, which is the van, so Diane is Horton, and her nickname is Woody. This leaves the compact car for Abby, so she is the salesperson, which means Diane is the carpenter. Eaton isn't the salesperson or the homemaker (6), so Eaton is the executive, Bruce. Carlyle isn't the homemaker (7), so Doyle is, and so Carlyle is the salesperson. Carlyle is not Lefty (10, salesperson) or Nicky (11, red car), so she is Curly. Eaton knows the salesperson (6), so he is not Lefty (10). So Eaton is Nicky, and so Nancy is Lefty.

Pg. 28-29

CHILDREN	FATHER	FATHER'S OCCUPATION	HOUSE POSITION	CHILD'S INTEREST
Sarah Quinlan	Fritz	bricklayer	3	mystery writer
Tammy Orthman	Jules	electrician	5	zookeeper
Udall Pierce	Homer	accountant	2	karate teacher
Vincent Roth	Ian	carpenter	4	X-ray technician
Walter Nelson	Gerhard	detective	1	locksmith

Since there are only two girls, the Nelson child is a boy (8), as is the Pierce child (3) and the Roth child (1). Then the Orthman and Quinlan children are girls. The future mystery writer (10) and the future zookeeper (4) are girls, so the other children are boys. The Pierce boy's interest is not in being a locksmith (3) or an X-ray technician (13), so he hopes to be a karate teacher. Fritz, whose child is a girl (8), is not the accountant or the detective (5, boys), the carpenter (6), or the electrician (8), so he is the bricklayer. Then the girls' fathers are the bricklayer and the electrician (8), so the boys' fathers are the accountant, the carpenter, and the detective. The would-be locksmith's father is not the accountant (12) or the carpenter (6), so he is the detective. All five houses are included in clues 9 and 2, although there isn't enough information to identify the order; Orthman, Ian, Gerhard, Udall, Quinlan, with Udall living in either the second or the fourth house. Using the information we already have, we can relist these, including the information of whether a boy or a girl lives there: Orthman (girl), Ian (boy), Gerhard, Udall (boy), Quinlan (girl). Since the girls are accounted for, Gerhard's child is a boy. Then we have Orthman (girl), Ian (boy), Gerhard (boy), Udall (boy), Quinlan (girl). Homer's child is a boy (1), so Homer is Udall's father. Then Jules is a girl's father, so he is the electrician. His daughter is not the future mystery writer (14), so she is the future zookeeper, and Fritz's daughter is the future mystery writer. Roth's son is not Udall (1, Homer) or Walter (15), so he is Vincent. The carpenter's house is at least the third house (6), and at least one of the other boys lives in a house before this house (6, locksmith). The boys whose fathers are the accountant and the detective both live on one end of the row (5), so this end has to be the left end. The future locksmith's house is before the accountant's house (12), so the accountant's house is the second house, and the future locksmith's house is the first. As stated earlier, Udall lives in the second or the fourth house. If he lives in the fourth, then Orthman, a girl, lives in the first (2), a contradiction. So Udall lives in the second house, Ian lives in the fourth, and Orthman lives in the fifth (2). Since Homer is Udall's father, and since a boy lives in the first house, then Sarah lives on the other side of Udall—that is, in the third house (11). Orthman, a girl, lives in the fifth house and, since Sarah lives in the third house, Tammy lives in the fifth house. Gerhard and Quinlan live on either side of Udall (9). A boy lives in the first house, and Quinlan is a girl, so Quinlan lives in the third house, and Gerhard lives in the first. Since the carpenter's child is a boy, this makes Ian the carpenter. We will now relist the houses according to the information we have so far.

1	2	3	4	5
	Udall	Sarah		Tammy
		Quinlan		Orthman
Gerhard	Homer		Ian	
detective	accountant		carpenter	
locksmith				

Then Pierce lives in the second house (3), and Fritz lives in the third house (6), so Jules lives in the fifth house. All last names except Walter's are accounted for, so Walter is Nelson. Walter's father is not the carpenter (7), so Vincent's father is, and Walter's father is the detective. The only future occupation unaccounted for is Vincent's, so he hopes to be the X-ray technician.

Pg. 30-31

NAME	CADDY	CAP	SCORE	POSITION
Portia Castor	Ina	violet	70	4th
Queenie Ebber	Hera	orange	71	5th
Ramona Barlow	Faye	yellow	68	2nd
Sherry Arthur	Jan	maroon	69	1st
Thelma Dinkman	Gwen	white	66	3rd

Sherry, Barlow, and the golfer in the orange cap knew each other before today (1), but the golfer with the lowest score and Ina's golfer did not know any of the others before today (1). This accounts for all five people. Then Hera's golfer, Ramona, and the golfer who teed off first today (4) are Sherry, Barlow, and the golfer in the orange cap, and Castor (4) is either the golfer with the lowest score or Ina's golfer. Also, Gwen's golfer, who did not practice putting yesterday morning (5) then must be the golfer with the lowest score or Ina's golfer. Since she is Gwen's golfer, she is not Ina's, so she is the golfer with the lowest score. Also, Queenie, Arthur, and the golfer who wears the yellow cap (3) are Sherry, Barlow, and the golfer in the orange cap. Summarizing what has been said so far, we have:

- Gwen's golfer scored 66.
- Castor is Gwen's golfer or Ina's golfer.
- Gwen's golfer and Ina's golfer did not know anyone else before today.
- Sherry Barlow, and orange cap = Queenie, Arthur, and yellow cap = Hera's golfer, Ramona, and 1st tee-off = women who know each other.

This list will be referred to below as *. Since Sherry, Queenie, and Ramona are the women who know each other (*), Portia is either Ina's or Gwen's golfer (*). She is not Gwen's golfer (5), so she is Ina's. Then the fifth woman, Thelma, is Gwen's golfer, who scored 66 (*). Then Castor is either Portia or Thelma (*). Thelma, who scored 66, did not wear the maroon cap (5, Gwen), the orange cap or the yellow cap (*), or the violet cap (7), so she wore the white cap. Portia didn't wear the maroon cap (5) or the orange or yellow cap (*), so she wore the violet cap. Faye's golfer shot 66 or 68 (6) but not 66 (Gwen's golfer), so she shot 68, and Queenie shot 71 (6). Portia didn't shoot 68 (Ina's golfer, not Faye's) or 69 (7, violet cap), so she shot 70. Then the woman who teed off second shot 68 (7) and so she is Faye's golfer. Thelma didn't tee off first (*) or second (Gwen's golfer, not Faye's). Combining clues 2 and 5, Thelma (Gwen's golfer) teed off ahead of both Portia and Ebber, so she didn't tee off fourth or fifth. Then she teed off third. Then Portia teed off fourth and Ebber teed off fifth (2, 5). Queenie, who shot 71, is not Faye's golfer (score 68) or Jan's golfer (8), so she is Hera's golfer. This then gives us Sherry, Barlow, and orange cap = Queenie, Ramona, and first tee-off (*), so Sherry teed off first. This also leaves us with Barlow and orange cap = Queenie and Ramona. Queenie, whose score was 71, didn't tee off second (68 score), so she teed off fifth, which means Queenie is Ebber. Then Ramona teed off second, so Ramona is Faye's golfer and shot 68. This leaves Sherry as the woman whose caddy is Jan and who shot 69. Since we previously knew that Barlow and orange cap = Queenie and Ramona, and since Queenie is Ebber, we now have that Ramona is Barlow and Queenie wears the orange cap. Then Sherry is Arthur (*). Since Arthur doesn't wear the yellow cap (*), Barlow wears it, and Arthur wears the maroon cap. Portia is not Dinkman (7, violet cap), so she is Castor, and so Thelma is Dinkman.

Pg. 32-33

NAME	FLOWER	SPECIAL TREATMENT	PRIZE
Anne Brown	rose	music	1st
Betty Smith	lily	sun	special award
Carol Felding	orchid	talk	honorable mention
Edith Lucas	violet	moving	2nd
Mary Chorn	tulip	solitude	3rd
Vera Dorman	dahlia	poetry	grand award

Mary isn't Smith (1), Lucas (1, 6), Felding (1, 4), Dorman (1, 5), or Brown (1, 7), so she is Chorn. The grand award winner wasn't the orchid, rose, or tulip (2), nor was it the lily or violet (8), so it was the dahlia, and it had poetry read to it (8). The violet won second prize and the orchid won honorable mention (12). The tulip didn't win first prize (2) or the special award (10), so it won third prize. The rose, which was entered by Brown (7), didn't win the special award (2), so it won first prize. Then the lily won the special award, so it was kept in the sun (11). Vera's entry won a higher prize than the rose (2), so Vera's entry won the grand award. Carol's flower placed lower than the tulip (10), so it was the orchid or the lily. It wasn't the lily (9, sun), so it was the orchid. Anne plays music to her flowers (9), and Edith moves her flowers around (3). Carol's method wasn't solitude or sun (9), so it was talking. Mary doesn't leave her flowers in the sun a lot (11), so her method is to leave the plants in solitude, and so Betty leaves hers in the sun. Then Betty entered the lily. Betty is not Brown (7, rose), Dorman (9, sun), Felding (4), or Lucas (6, special award), so she is Smith. Brown, whose rose took first prize, is not Carol (orchid), Vera (dahlia), or Edith (3, 7), so she is Anne. Lucas' flower took a prize higher than third (6, tulip) but not grand award (6) or first prize (Brown), so it took second prize, and so Lucas entered the violet. Lucas isn't Mary Chorn, so she is Edith. Then Mary Chorn entered the tulip. Carol isn't Dorman (9), so she is Felding, and so Vera is Dorman.

Pg. 34-35

NAME	TEAM	OCCUPATION	POSITION
Art Newton	Rollers	police officer	2nd
Bob Payton	Scorers	teacher	4th
Chuck Renalt	Jinxes	plumber	5th
Dave Miller	Anchors	cashier	3rd
Ed Oliver	Toppers	firefighter	6th
Frank Queen	Framers	manager	1st

Bob isn't Oliver (1). Bob's average is and has always been a steady 190 (1), so Bob isn't Miller (5), Newton (12), Queen (11), or Renault (7). So Bob is Payton. Art is the police officer (8), and Dave is the cashier (9). The firefighter is not Bob or Frank (4) or Chuck (8), so he is Ed, and his team ended up in sixth place (4). The Jinxes finished fifth and the Anchors finished third (10). The Scorers didn't finish first or second (6) or sixth (3), so they finished fourth. The Rollers didn't finish first or sixth (6), so they finished second, which means Frank's team finished first (6), and Frank is the manager (2). His team isn't the Toppers (2), so it is the Framers, and the firefighter's team is the Toppers. Chuck's team ended in fifth or sixth place (3) but not in sixth place (Ed, the firefighter), so it finished in fifth place. So Chuck is on the Jinxes. Chuck is not the public school teacher (8), so Bob Payton is, and so Chuck is the plumber. Queen isn't Art or Chuck (8) or Ed (8, firefighter) or Dave (9, 11), so he is Frank. Newton, who is on the Rollers (12), is not Dave (9, 12), Ed (Toppers), or Chuck (Jinxes), so he is Art. Renalt is not Ed (7) or Dave (7, 9), so he is Chuck. Ed, whose team finished in sixth place, is not Miller (5), so Ed is Oliver, and Dave is Miller. Miller isn't on the Scorers (5), so Payton is, and Miller is on the Anchors.

Pg. 36-37

NAME	MATH	UNIVERSITY	HOME CITY
Amy Jackson	computer programming	University of Nebraska	New York City
Brad Garrett	measure theory	Wayne State University	Denver
Carl Landon	probability theory	MIT	Chicago
Dorothy Horner	game theory	University of Denver	Seattle
Elaine King	number theory	UCLA	Kansas City
Fred Iwasi	vector spaces	Tulane	Phoenix

(Note: For clue 1, a Webster's dictionary will give the locations of the universities, and a straight-line measure of a map will give approximate air distances between cities.) Carl studies probability theory (6), and Elaine studies number theory (4). Fred doesn't study computer programming (8, female) or game theory or measure theory (6), so he studies uses of vector spaces. Jackson doesn't specialize in game, measure, number, or probability theory (6) or vector spaces (6, Fred), so she specializes in computer programming and is, therefore, from New York City (8). She doesn't attend MIT or Wayne (1), or University of Denver (8), or Tulane or UCLA (9), so she attends University of Nebraska. The females are Jackson (above), Horner (2), and King (10), so the males are Garrett, Iwasi, and Landon. The person who studies game theory is from Seattle (5) and is a female (3). She isn't Amy (3) or Elaine (number theory), so she is Dorothy. Then Amy, the only female unmatched with her specialty, is the one who studies computer programming (8), so she is Jackson. This leaves Brad, whose home city is Denver (2), to specialize in measure theory. King isn't Dorothy (5, Seattle), so she is Elaine. Then Dorothy is Horner. Landon attends MIT (4), and Iwasi attends Tulane (10). Dorothy Horner doesn't attend Wayne (11) or UCLA (9, Seattle), so she attends University of Denver. Elaine King doesn't attend Wayne (11), so she attends UCLA. Then Elaine is not from Phoenix (1), so she is from Chicago or Kansas City. Going from west to east, the home cities are Seattle, Phoenix, Denver, Kansas City, Chicago, and New York City. Since Amy Jackson is from New York City and attends University of Nebraska, the farthest east the home city of the MIT student can be is Chicago. Then Elaine, the UCLA student can't be from Chicago (9), so she is from Kansas City, and the MIT student, Landon, is from Chicago. Then Brad (Denver) is not Landon. He isn't Iwasi

(10), so he is Garrett. Fred isn't from Chicago (7), so he isn't Landon. So Fred is Iwasi, and Carl is Landon. Since all other home cities are accounted for, Fred is from Phoenix. And since all other universities are accounted for, Brad attends Wayne.

Pg. 38-39

HORSE	JOCKEY	TRAINER	OWNER	LAST TRACK	COLOR	PLACE
Apollo	Klinger	Raymond	Ulrich	Belmont	chestnut	6th
Beauty	Geyer	Oster	Sampson	Hialeah	amber	3rd
Charmer	Jason	Quell	Werner	Arlington	tan	1st
Dazzler	Ivers	Manning	Tuller	Santa Anita	black	2nd
Enchanter	Harmon	Pauling	Yolder	Churchill Downs	white	5th
Fascinator	Lehman	Newman	Viner	Pimlico	gray	4th

Apollo's jockey wasn't Harmon, Ivers, or Lehman (8) or Jason or Geyer (3), so she or he was Klinger. Yolder, Viner, and Sampson are women (9). Ulrich (11) and Werner (12) are men. Dazzler's owner is a man (5) but isn't Werner or Ulrich (5), so he is Tuller. Apollo's owner is male (13, Klinger) but isn't Werner (12), so he is Ulrich. Werner doesn't own Beauty or Fascinator (12) or Enchanter (7), so he owns Charmer. Ivers rode for a male owner (20), but he or she didn't ride Charmer (8), so Ivers rode Dazzler. Geyer, who rode for a female owner (17), didn't ride Charmer (male owner). Also, Charmer wasn't ridden by Harmon or Lehman (8), so Jason rode Charmer. Beauty wasn't ridden by Harmon or Lehman (8), so Geyer rode Beauty. Combining clues 6, 1, and 4, respectively, we get a complete ranking of the way the horses finished in today's race: 1, tan; 2, Tuller; 3, Beauty; 4, Newman; 5, Churchill Downs; 6, chestnut. This will be referred to below as *. Combining this information with clue 10, we have the following: 1, tan; 2, black; 3, amber; 4 and 5, white and gray; 6, chestnut. This will be referred to below as **. Then Dazzler (Tuller's horse) is black, and Beauty is amber (*, **). The hard-to-handle horses are Apollo, Beauty, and Charmer (8). Beauty finished third (*), so Apollo and Charmer finished first and sixth (15). Charmer didn't finish sixth (16, Jason), so Charmer finished first, and Apollo finished sixth. Then Charmer is tan and Apollo is chestnut (*). Enchanter is not gray (7), so Fascinator is gray, and Enchanter is white. Newman, who trained the fourth-place horse (*), did not train Enchanter (13), so Enchanter didn't finish fourth. Then Enchanter finished fifth, and so last raced at Churchill Downs (*), and Fascinator finished fourth (and so was trained by Newman). Viner's horse last raced at Pimlico (18). The horse which last raced at Hialeah isn't owned by Werner (6, tan), Tuller (6), Ulrich (11), or Yolder (14), so it is owned by Sampson. This horse is not Enchanter (Churchill Downs) or Fascinator (11), so Beauty raced last at Hialeah (and so is owned by Sampson). Then Viner owns either Enchanter or Fascinator, but she doesn't own Enchanter (Churchill Downs), so she owns Fascinator, which leaves Yolder to own Enchanter. Manning didn't train Apollo (11, Ulrich), Beauty (11, Hialeah), Charmer (22, tan), or Enchanter (21, Yolder), so he trained Dazzler. Pauling didn't train Apollo (3), Beauty (3, Geyer), or Charmer (3, Jason), so she (3) trained Enchanter. Quell didn't train Apollo (19) or Beauty (17, Geyer), so he or she trained Charmer. Beauty's trainer wasn't Raymond (17, Geyer), so Raymond trained Apollo, and Oster trained Beauty. Harmon wasn't Fascinator's jockey (18, Viner), so Lehman was, and Harmon rode Enchanter. Charmer didn't race last at Belmont or Santa Anita (19, Quell), so Charmer's last race was at Arlington. Dazzler's last race wasn't at Belmont (6, Tuller), so Apollo's was, and Dazzler last raced at Santa Anita.

Pg. 40-41

NAME	AGE	WEIGHT (kg)	HEIGHT (cm)	BIRTH MONTH	DATE OF BIRTH
Arturo Juarez	13	59	167	5	11th
Bernardo Lee	19	82	182	6	12th
Chi-Wei Houh	25	50	155	4	10th
Dominic Guernari	17	77	187	11	22nd
Elseyn Kung	20	56	168	8	4th
Francesca Ito	16	48	163	7	3rd

Arturo's weight is 59 kg (1), Dominic's is 77 (4), and Houh's is 50 (5). Francesca, who is not Houh (6), weighs 48 kg (6). Then Francesca's age is 16 (6), and Houh's age is 25 (6). Chi-Wei's month of birth is April (7), and her age is 25 (7). Then Chi-Wei is Houh, so the day of the month she was born is the 10th (5), and her height is 155 cm (5). Dominic's height is 187 cm (4), and his month of birth is November (4). Kung's height is 168 cm (3), and his or her birth month is August (3). Elseyn's age is 20 and she was born on the 4th of the month (13). Lee's birth month is not May, July, or November (8), so it is June. Elseyn's is not May or July (8), or June (8, Lee), so it is August. Then Elseyn is Kung, so her weight is 56 kg (3). This leaves 82 kg for Bernardo's weight, 182 cm for his height (9), and June for his birth month (9), which means he is Lee. He is not 13 or 16 or 17 (10), so he is 19. The only ages below Lee's, 19, are 13, 16, and 17, so these are the ages of Juarez, Ito, and Guernari, respectively (10). Then Francesca, 16, is Ito. Dominic, whose height is 187 cm, is not Juarez, who is 13 (2), so he is Guernari, 17. Then Arturo is Juarez, 13. Juarez' and Ito's heights are the only ones unaccounted for, 163 cm and 167 cm. Since Juarez is the taller (11), his height is 167 cm, and Ito's is 163 cm. Arturo was born on the 3rd or 11th (1). But he is the youngest, so he wasn't born on the 3rd (12). So Arturo was born on the 11th. Then Dominic was born on the 22nd (4). Bernardo wasn't born on the 3rd (9), so Francesca was, and so Bernardo was born on the 12th. Juarez (the youngest) was born in May and Ito (born on the 3rd) was born in July (12).

Pg. 42-43

PLAYER	POSITION	AGE	ORDER JOINED	MARRIED OR SINGLE
José Edwards	center field	22	5th	married
Kevin Grant	2nd base	23	9th	single
Lou Abbott	left field	25	8th	married
Mike Carter	shortstop	21	7th	single
Neil Baker	catcher	33	1st	single
Otis Horner	pitcher	27	6th	married
Paul Irving	right field	26	4th	single
Quincy Drake	1st base	28	2nd	married
Rick Fraser	3rd base	34	3rd	single

Note: * below refers to the second paragraph of the problem. "MS" means "the first person is married, but the second is single;" "SM" means "the first person is single, but the second is married." Otis, the pitcher (1), is married (13). Then the catcher is single (14). The first names of the other married men are Lou and José (12) and Quincy (13, *). The last names of the married men are Horner and Drake (12), Edwards (11), and Abbott (13, *). All other players are single (14). Rick is not Abbott (SM), Baker (15), Carter (2, 3), Drake (3), Edwards (SM), Grant (15), Horner (SM), or Irving (15), so he is Fraser. Mike is not Abbott (SM), Baker (15), Drake or Edwards (SM), Grant (15), Horner (SM), or Irving (15), so he is Carter. Lou, who is married, is not Drake (12), Edwards (15), or Horner (5), so he is Abbott. José, also married, is not Drake or Horner (12), so he is Edwards. Irving is not Kevin (16), Neil (18), or Otis or Quincy (SM), so he is Paul. Baker is not Kevin (16) or Otis or Quincy (SM), so he is Neil. Grant is not Otis or Quincy (SM), so he is Kevin. The only ages divisible by 3 are 21, 27, and 33, and 2/3 of these are 14, 18, and 22. So the catcher is 33, and the fifth man to join the team is 22 (8). Since Paul Irving is the oldest of the outfielders (17), he has to be at least 23, so he is not the fifth man to join the team, who is 22. He also wasn't the sixth (18) or one of the first three (3) to join. Since he is not the left fielder (19), he wasn't one of the last three to join (2). So he was the fourth man to join the team. He is not the left fielder (19, Paul) or the center fielder (21), so he is the right fielder. The only age divisible by 4 is 28, and 3/4 of this is 21, so the first baseman is 28, and the shortstop is 21 (4). Then the third baseman, who is the oldest of the infielders (17), has to be 33 or 34. He is not 33 (catcher), so he is 34. Since the shortstop is 21, and since Paul Irving is the oldest outfielder (17), Paul is at least 25. Then the first man to join the team has to be 33 or 34 (9, Paul 4th to join). If this man is 34, then Quincy is 29 (9), not one of the given ages. So the first man to join is 33 (the catcher), Quincy is 28 (the first baseman) (9), and Paul Irving is 26 (9). The last three men to join the team were the left fielder, Mike Carter, and Kevin Grant (2). Since Lou Abbott joined after Mike Carter but before Kevin Grant (22), Lou Abbott is the left fielder. Then Carter, Abbott, and Grant were the seventh, eighth, and ninth, respectively, to join the team (22, 2). Since Irving, the right fielder, is single, the other two outfielders are married (14). The positions of all married men except Edwards are already identified, so José Edwards is the center fielder. Kevin, the ninth to join the team, is not the catcher (first to join), and he doesn't play third base (6) or shortstop (20), so he plays second base. Rick is not the catcher (3) or the shortstop (20), so he plays third base (and is 34 years old). Mike Carter (seventh to join), is not the catcher (first to join), so Neil Baker is, and Mike plays shortstop (21 years old). Since Paul Irving is 26, Neil Baker is at least 28 (18). Neil is not 28 (Quincy) or 34 (Rick), so he is 33 (the catcher). Since the catcher was the first to join the team, Rick was either the second or the third (3). Since Rick is 34, the oldest player on the team, he was the third to join (23), and Drake was the second (3, 23). Since Paul Irving is 26, the sum of the ages of Horner and Abbott, the left fielder, is 52 (19). The only ages left which have this sum are 25 and 27, so Horner and Abbott are 25 and 27. Then Quincy, who is 28, is not Horner, so he is Drake, which leaves Otis to be Horner, who is 25 or 27 (as is Abbott). The men who are 28, 33, and 34 were the first three to join the team, so the sixth man to join, who is older than Irving (18), has to be 27. This person is not José Edwards, the center fielder, since Edwards is younger than Irving, 26, the right fielder (21), so Horner was the sixth, and Edwards the fifth, to join the team, which also means that Horner is 27, Edwards is 22, and Abbott is 25 (above). This leaves Grant to be 23.

Pg. 44-45

LAST NAME	WIFE	HUSBAND	WIFE'S COSTUME	HUSBAND'S COSTUME	STREET
Uster	Beth	Len	Cinderella	Hansel	Cedar
Vincent	Esther	Gerhard	Queen of Sheba	Prince Charming	Redwood
Wyler	Cornelia	Reuben	Snow White	Napoleon	Elm
Yang	Anita	Isaac	Sleeping Beauty	Frankenstein	Maple
Zorbet	Driselda	Terrance	Gretel	Moses	Chestnut

Isaac doesn't live on Chestnut, Elm, or Redwood (1d) or on Cedar (11), so he lives on Maple. His last name isn't Uster, Wyler, or Zorbet (1b) or Vincent (3, 4), so it is Yang. Cornelia doesn't live on Maple (1e), so her last name isn't Yang. Neither is it Vincent or Zorbet (1a) or Uster (9, 10), so it is Wyler. Esther is not Uster (10), Yang (1a), or Zorbet (1c), so she is Vincent. Anita is not Uster or Zorbet (1a), so she is Yang, Isaac's wife. Beth isn't Zorbet (1c), so she is Uster. Then Driselda is Zorbet. The Zorbets don't live on Cedar (1e, Driselda), Elm (5), or Redwood (1f), so they live on Chestnut. Cornelia Wyler doesn't live on Cedar or Redwood (1e), so she lives on Elm. The Vincents don't live on Cedar (3, 4), so they live on Redwood, and the Usters live on Cedar. Beth isn't married to Gerhard or Terrance (1d, Cedar) or Reuben (1b, Uster), so she is married to Len. Her costume wasn't Gretel or Snow White (3, Cedar), Queen of Sheba (6, Uster), or Sleeping Beauty (12, Len), so it was Cinderella. Moses isn't the husband of Beth or Anita (3, Cedar and Maple) or Cornelia (9) or Esther (9, 10), so he is married to Driselda. Frankenstein isn't married to Beth (6, Uster), Cornelia (15, Elm), or Esther (13), so he is married to Anita. Napoleon isn't married to Beth (6, Uster) or Esther Vincent (4, Redwood), so he is married to Cornelia. Terrance isn't married to Cornelia Wyler (1c) or to Esther (13), so he is married to Driselda. Gerhard isn't married to Cornelia Wyler (1c), so he is married to Esther, and so Reuben is married to Cornelia. Gretel is not Anita (2b), Cornelia (14, Reuben), or Esther Vincent (4, Redwood), so she is Driselda (and so is married to Moses). We already know that

Mrs. Uster dressed as Cinderella, so Hansel was not married to Sleeping Beauty or Snow White (6). He wasn't married to Queen of Sheba (7), so he was married to Cinderella. This leaves Mr. Vincent to be dressed as Prince Charming. The Usters are Cinderella and Hansel, so Prince Charming isn't married to Sleeping Beauty or Snow White (6), so he is married to Queen of Sheba. Mrs. Yang is not Snow White (2c), so Mrs. Wyler is, and Mrs. Yang is Sleeping Beauty.

Pg. 46-47

LAST NAME	WIFE	HUSBAND	STREET	PARTY	DRINK
Aston	Helene	Orville	Talbot	New Year's Eve	punch
Barler	Freda	Morton	Stoddard	Halloween	iced tea
Cauchy	Julia	Kermit	Rawlins	Independence Day	lemonade
Dick	Ginny	Norbert	Palmer	Valentine's Day	coffee
Eggler	Ilene	Leon	Quinton	St. Patrick's Day	fruit juice

The Stoddard couple gave the Halloween party and served iced tea (5). The Egglers gave the St. Patrick's Day party (6), and they live on Quinton (2). The Dicks gave the Valentine's Day party (4). The Palmer couple didn't give the Independence Day party or the New Year's Eve party (9), so they gave the Valentine's Day party (and so they are the Dicks). Orville and his wife gave the New Year's Eve party (10). They don't live on Rawlins (11, Orville), so they live on Talbot. Then the couple on Rawlins had the Independence Day party. Orville, on Talbot, is not Barler (11), Cauchy (14), Dick (Palmer), or Eggler (Quinton), so he is Aston. The Barlers don't live on Rawlins (11), so they live on Stoddard, and the Cauchys live on Rawlins. Mr. Barler is not Leon or Norbert (8) or Kermit (12, Stoddard), so he is Morton. Mr. Eggler is not Kermit (13, St. Patrick's Day party) or Norbert (3), so he is Leon. Helene doesn't live on Palmer (4, Dick), Quinton (13, St. Patrick's Day party), Rawlins (15), or Stoddard (12), so she lives on Talbot (and so she is Mrs. Aston). Helene and Orville Aston don't serve coffee (7), fruit juice (17), or lemonade (3), so they serve punch. Mrs. Barler, who serves iced tea, is not Ilene or Julia (1) or Ginny (7), so she is Freda. Ginny isn't Mrs. Cauchy (7) or Mrs. Eggler (16, Leon), so she is Mrs. Dick, and she serves coffee (7). Mrs. Eggler doesn't serve lemonade (3), so Mrs. Cauchy does, and so Mrs. Eggler serves fruit juice. Norbert isn't Mr. Cauchy (3, lemonade), so he is Mr. Dick, and Kermit is Mr. Cauchy. Ilene isn't Mrs. Cauchy (15, Rawlins), so she is Mrs. Eggler, and Julia is Mrs. Cauchy.

Pg. 48-49

LAST NAME	CHILD	MOTHER	FATHER	CITY	STATE
Allan	Gerald	Marla	Reuben	Willie	Idaho
Boncher	Julie	Olive	Quentin	Ulrich	Alabama
Crachy	Frank	Leah	Todd	Zebra	Kansas
Dorkea	Iris	Neva	Stuart	Valley	Tennessee
Effer	Helga	Kitty	Porter	Yellow	Ohio

Olive isn't married to Porter (10, 7), Reuben (10, 6), Stuart (10, 8), or Todd (15), so she is married to Quentin. They don't live in Idaho (10, 5), Kansas (10, 16), Ohio (1, Olive), or Tennessee (2, Olive), so they live in Alabama. They aren't the Allans (10, 8), the Crachys (11), the Dorkeas (10, 5), or the Effers (10, 6), so they are the Bonchers. From clue 3, Ulrich is not in Idaho, Kansas, Ohio, or Tennessee, so it is in Alabama. Helga doesn't live in Alabama (2), so her last name isn't Boncher. Neither is it Allan (14, 8), Crachy (11, male), or Dorkea (14, 16), so it is Effer. Iris is not Olive's daughter (10, 7), so her last name isn't Boncher. Also it isn't Allan (7) or Crachy (11, male), so it is Dorkea. Kitty doesn't live in Valley (2), Willie (4), or Zebra (9), so she lives in Yellow. Neither Marla nor Neva lives in Zebra (2), so Leah lives there. Leah's last name is not Dorkea (2), Effer (2, Helga), or Allan (8), so it is Crachy. Zebra isn't in Idaho or Tennessee (11) or Ohio (3), so it is in Kansas. Leah's (11, Crachy) and Marla's (13) children are boys, so Olive Boncher's child is the remaining girl, Julie, and Marla is Mrs. Allan. Stuart doesn't live in Willie or Yellow (9) or Zebra (8, Leah) so he lives in Valley. Marla Allan doesn't live in Valley (8, Stuart) or Yellow (Kitty), so she lives in Willie. Then Neva lives in Valley and so she is married to Stuart. Helga Effer doesn't live in Valley (14, 8, Stuart), so she lives in Yellow (and so her mother is Kitty). Then Iris lives in Valley. Reuben is not the father of Helga (6, Effer) or Frank (6), so he is Gerald's father. Frank doesn't live in Willie (9), so he lives in Zebra, and Gerald lives in Willie. Todd doesn't live in Yellow (9), so he lives in Zebra, and Porter lives in Yellow. The Dorkea family doesn't live in Idaho (5) or Ohio (3, Valley), so they live in Tennessee. Reuben doesn't live in Ohio (12, Marla), so he lives in Idaho. Then the Effers live in Ohio.